VERY ADVANCED
DRIVING

PUBLISHER'S NOTE

Tom Topper's earlier Paperfront "Learning to Drive In Pictures", was acclaimed by "The Times", "The Daily Telegraph", "The Sun", "The Daily Mirror", "Woman's Own" and others.

The sales quickly exceeded six figures and (quite exceptionally) more publicity was accorded when the second edition appeared by "The Daily Mail" and "Woman's Own" (again). It is used in hundreds of driving schools and in an increasing number of colleges where youngsters learn the theory before reaching Test age. Every succeeding edition is updated.

The book carries a money back guarantee if a reader fails his Test or does not agree that it is the greatest book on learning to drive.

This is the fifth huge revised edition of "Very Advanced Driving". Tom's continuing enthusiastic post-bag and impressive sales confirm our belief that his fascinating approach to safe driving through thinking and positioning will long remain the standard text. A few extracts demonstrate his style:

"snarl-ups . . . are made much worse by drivers who sit . . . with their motoring-minds vacant."

"a hoot in time may change disaster into breathing space."

"consideration for others is the essence of good driving manners."

"maintain a cocoon of safe-area all around you."

"never pass in this world by risking passing into the next."

"the greatest quality in driving is having nerves of steel; the supreme folly is to take advantage of them."

"think while learning; it is more productive than when you are lying up in Mayday."

VERY ADVANCED DRIVING

BY

A. TOM TOPPER

PAPERFRONTS

**ELLIOT RIGHT WAY BOOKS
KINGSWOOD, SURREY, U.K.**

CONDITIONS OF SALE
This book shall only be sold, lent or hired for profit, trade, or otherwise in its original binding, except where special permission has been granted by the Publishers.

Every effort is made to ensure that Paperfronts and Right Way Books are accurate, and that the information given in them is correct. However, information can become out of date, and author's or printers' errors can creep in. This book is sold, therefore, on the condition that neither Author nor Publisher can be held legally responsible for the consequences of any error or omission there may be.

Made and Printed in Great Britain by Robert Hartnoll Ltd, Bodmin, Cornwall.

CONTENTS

Pedestrians. Nose-To-Tail. Nose-To-Tail "Grass Roots" Principle. For Turning Left An "Unofficial" Signal May Be Easier. Making Visual Safety When You Helpfully Stop For People. Make Time While Green Lasts. Joining "Through" Routes From Side Roads At "T" Junctions. Turning Left, Joining A Main Road With Two Lanes Each Way. Turning Right, Joining A Main Road With Two Lanes Each Way. Crossing "Through" Routes. "Doubling" When Turning Right On To A Road With Two Lanes Each Way. Chock A Block Through Route Bedlam. Zebra Crossing Safety. Headlight Flashing. Headlight Flashing Customs. Traffic Light Knowledge. The Green Pelican. Using Green Efficiently. Going Fast Through Green On Wide Empty "Through" Routes. One-Ways. First Example Of The Advantages Of Using The Lane Least Likely To Be Held Up. One-Way Underpasses. Second Example Of Using The Lane Least Likely To Be Held Up. Multi-Lane City Roundabouts. Third Example Of Using The Lane Least Likely To Be Held Up. The "Road Narrows" Problem. Approaching One-Way Streets. Traffic Flow. Easy-Way For One-Ways. Town Streets. Keeping Your Distance. How A Signal Can Banish Doubt. Do You Always Look Under Parked Cars? Hooting On Behalf Of Others. Swarming Pedestrians. Hidden Monsters. Blind Spots. Systemising A Safety Eye Approach To Junctions. The Deadly Blind Junction. The Danger Of Stalling. Positioning – Safety's Supreme Ally. Stopping And Parking. Pedestrians Are Crackers. Motto For Reversing – Don't. Town Bottlenecks. The Moving Obstruction.

low My Leader Overtaking. The World Of Difference Between An Accelerating Pass And Passing With Speed In Hand. Telling Someone In Front He Should Have The Chance To Pass First. "Prison". The Russian Roulette Pass.

6. BAD WEATHER 113
Using Headlights In Poor Daytime Visibility. Fog. Surprise Patches Of Fog. Spitting Rain. What To Do. Cloudbursts, Torrential Rain. Overtaking In Rain. Sunshine. Dazzle In Your Mirror From The Sun. When Dazzled Yourself.

7. NIGHT DRIVING 117
Twilight Or Dawn, Or Poor Light. In Towns. Helping People At Junctions. More Tips For Towns At Night. Following Other People. In The Country. When Leading A Traffic Stream Through Countryside. The Permanently Dipped Or "Dippy" Driver. Passing Cyclists Or Small Obstructions At Night. Speed In The Dark. Dazzling. Overtaking At Night. Signals For Night-Time Overtaking. Dim Headlamps.

8. MOTORWAY DRIVING 122
Which Lane? Do Not Follow Directly. Motorway Mirrors. Right Indicators For Overtaking. Speed Boggling. Drowsiness. Lane Discipline. Motorways In Bad Weather. Snow, Black (Invisible) Ice. Motorway Accidents. The "Psycho" Flash.

9. AUTOMATIC TRANSMISSION 128
Only The Right Foot. Reverse With The Right Foot. Check Your Advanced (Correct) Moving Off Procedure. Advanced Hill Starting Off. Traffic Queues. Pitfalls For Those Who Have To Chop And Change Between Manual And Automatic Cars.

10. SKIDDING 129
Can You Control Skids? Three Main Types Of Skid. Definition of Terms. Locked Brakes. Aquaplaning. Locked Brake Aquaplaning. Skids When Braking Hard. Prevent These Hard Braking Skids. Spotting A Mechanical Fault. How To Deal With Hard Braking Skids. An Extremely Rare Occurrence. So Far We Have Looked Mainly At Theory. Answers. An Amazing Skid. More About Surfaces. Wet. Traffic Dust, Oil And Wet. Loose Surfaces (Gravel, Wet Leaves, Mud, Etc.). Black (Invisible) Ice . . . The Surprise Killer. Snow Or Snow With Ice On Top. Over-Acceleration Skids. Starting From Rest. Uphills In Snow. Go Up It In Reverse. Over-Acceleration Skids At Faster Speeds. Sideslip Skids. Without

Warning The Car Ahead Suddenly Spins Off A Straight Road. Cornering Too Fast. So How Can The Fastest Cornering At The Limit Of Safety Be Achieved? The Limit of Adhesion. "Slow In, Fast Out". Preventing Sideslip Skids. The Technique Of Braking Into A Corner. Allowing Room For Error. When You Haven't Room To Allow Space For Error. Eliminating Sideslip Even On "Ice-Rink" Roads. Sweeping Wide Bends. Last Resorts. Catching A Sideslip In Its Early Stages. Too Late! A Sideslip Has Turned You Almost, Or Completely Round, Or The Car Is Spinning Further Round Than Just Backwards. Let Skidding Fools Miss You. Understeer And Oversteer.

LIST OF ILLUSTRATIONS

WATCH FOR THE CATCH IN
ADVANCED DRIVING !

Long before people talked about "advanced" driving my publishers brought out a book in two parts one of which dealt with "The Advanced Driver". The term advanced driver is now used widely.

Various courses and competitions give "passes" for "special ability". To obtain such "qualifications" can cost a lot of money and in my view they are hardly worth the paper on which they are written.

Unfortunately, one motive of many in getting these "passes" is the hope that others—including the insurance companies, some employers, and the courts—will think because they have the pass they are expert drivers. I am sure this does not fool many magistrates or our great British judges.

I fear that many who obtain these "passes" imagine themselves to be "road-Gods", superior to all the other, silly drivers, than which there is nothing more dangerous.

Diploma Mania

It is an age in which people have become obsessed by diplomas and bits of paper, yet everyone from the day they pass the simple government test should be learning to drive better by experience and the study of driving. That is what matters and not being able to swank some certificate or other. I have been a passenger with a number of "certified" drivers who have scared the life out of me. Nothing must be allowed (even unconsciously) to come before safety and thoughtfulness for other road users.

Mind Preparation

I hope to encourage you to think about and analyse your own driving, and to develop continuing enthusiasm for safe, happy motoring. "Very" advanced driving is largely commonsense based on safety for others laced with self preservation. But such commonsense has to be reflected upon, chewed over in the mind, if it is to become

11

"common" and automatic on today's appallingly dangerous roads.

You need to train your mind to meet emergencies, for only if knowledge and experience have become a part of your subconscious, will you have the ability, on which lives may depend, to react correctly and quickly enough during split second unexpected emergencies. It is the mind preparation—learning from and thinking about your experiences—that makes the right reaction "instinctive".

Positioning and Speed

Not all the boffins in Whitehall, nor all the clauses in the Highway Code, nor the whole lot of "passes" or driving certificates, speed limits, police cars and road engineers put together with anything else you like, can equal in importance the twin points which are so rarely stressed—positioning and relating speed to conditions.

Neither the one nor the other can save you, but the use of the both at once is the basis of the "Very" advanced driving which this book attempts to explain.

I

"THE OTHER IDIOT"

Many dead drivers would be living had they not stopped learning and thinking for themselves at driving test standard. Becoming "very" advanced is a personal challenge requiring continual and concentrated thinking effort.

WHAT IS AN IDIOT DRIVER MUMMY?

I make no apology for opening with a tilt at the ubiquitous "other idiot". Pompous as we all can be in excluding ourselves from this idiotic roll of honour, the fact is everyone makes mistakes; however, in this regard some people are habitués. A friend of my publishers, Roy Neal, himself an author, has even coined the breed "buppies". He points out that "buppy" people ever conform with conformity, that is they copy each other and strive to do the approved or accepted thing. Rarely, if ever, do they think for themselves. They may not all conform with each other but they usually fall into clearly defined groups. Thus stockbrokers with their pinstriped suits, bowler hats, furled umbrellas and buttonholes are as typical a group as are "the bingo brigade", another collection. There are lots of idiotic sub-groups of drivers. I will indicate a few types:

The Jealous Idiot

He accelerates when being overtaken but more exasperatingly slows up when he is not, seemingly doing everything he can to hold up other people's progress.

The Half-Witted Idiot

He weaves along apparently thinking about anything but what he is doing and he then has to make an abrupt stop when he has not noticed something in time. Some are erratic, plunging to the depths of sluggardliness at times, but expect them to be going flat out next minute. Others are distracted looking out for direction signs or the street

13

or property they are trying to find and will pull up, without drawing off the carriageway, regardless of inconvenience to those behind. They are selfish, sometimes dangerously.

The Nervous

They are abominably slow and apparently unable to digest what is happening round them. They may not realise how much anger builds up in the queue behind but they are human!

The "My Speed" Type

These idiots seem to have a set speed at which happiness overtakes them. It is the same whether the conditions are safe or a dangerous shopping area is at hand. Relentlessly they maintain "their" speed, holding up faster people on open roads perhaps but worse, a threat to life whenever they pass through crowded areas.

The Motorway "My Speed" Idiot

I quote from a Roy Neal letter on this subject.

"The Buppy People follow Anybody, Anything. They have to follow somebody or something, otherwise they'd get stuck on the hard shoulder, having no initiative of their own. . . .

"Friday night on the M.1 is merciless example. Friday night, contrary to the B.B.C.'s impression, is not music night, it's bleeting mad Buppies night as thousands of week-end commuters are spewn from London in nose-to-tail escape to country freedom.

"Ever been in a multiple pile-up? Odds are that if you use the M.1 northways on a Friday night—yes. There's more such pile-ups than ever reach a bye-line in the Muck-Binding Echo, let alone headlines in the national press.

"Twenty cars up ahead you can see the first glow of red brake lights. Sensibly you ease your own brakes on slowly, then quickly, as the column in front crunches to a halt.

"Unfortunately . . . somebody behind you has not been noticing those red lights . . . or else he thought it was a mobile knocking shop maybe? Either way, the upshot is that he cannot stop as quick as you can. If you are lucky, then he'll manage to swivel on to the hard shoulder and come to a halt lower down. If you ain't lucky, then pass this book on to somebody else, you won't be needing it.

"When it happened to me—there were three cars finished up astride the central reservation. Each one was an old banger! They just hadn't got the brakes to match the situation! Fact. It happened. So what the Hell were the three drivers doing in the fast lane bumper to bumper, with brakes that didn't stop so good?

"70 m.p.h.

"That's what.

"Talk about Buppy Drivers! It must have taken each driver up to half an hour apiece to pump their old crocks up to the said 70 m.p.h. Then they proceeded to stay in the fast lane. They couldn't have thought what they were doing . . . they must have just blindly followed their leaders—any bloody leader who happened to be handy???

"It ain't no secret that you should drive according to prevailing conditions is it? Does it have to be printed in black and white that the condition of the car counts as well?"

Good Drivers (Possibly "Very" Advanced Idiots?)

A man who overtakes leaving 18 inches clearance to his nearside (but several yards from traffic in the other direction) may be superb—or a B . . . F . . .! Only further clues will reveal. You judge people as you follow. The good ones rarely weave or dart in and out; braking is infrequent and turning round to talk taboo. Following them, you feel secure that they will warn of any problem and that you can guess their reaction in difficulty; "slow in danger, get moving when it is clear" is their motto.

In the mirror again you will notice that the good never meander, especially police cars! During danger they fall noticeably further back, only coming close when there may be a possible overtaking opportunity. You can often tell if a police driver is following by the way he handles his car.

Other Good Drivers

The twenty-ton lorry, cement mixer or the vintage Bentley will rarely hit you—these drivers are mainly professionals—beware the ten-year-old family car, local grocery van and the young speed-merchant in his racer! Watch the learner out for the first day who will likely jam on the brakes if the gear stick shakes!

The "very" advanced driver will wish to avoid being

15

identifiable with an idiot group. He continually plans his advanced positioning methods as traffic problems dictate. I stress this because it is vital to guard against having irrevocably set ideas for this or that situation; a continuing review is essential throughout your driving lifetime. New better thinking must be allowed to bubble out.

With decisions made instantly during driving, sometimes hardest of all is stopping oneself acting knowingly wrongly, i.e. taking chances. Self-discipline, the scarcest, yet most essential good driving ingredient is your only guardian.

SLOW DOWN BY 10%

As an experiment, next time you drive cut usual speeds by 10% and keep your eyes flashing, trying to watch every danger possibility. It can be frightening to discover the extent to which we all miss obvious potential hazards at higher speeds, even if we do not consider ourselves fast drivers.

RUNNING COMMENTARY

Running a commentary out loud about where danger lurks, why and how you are counteracting each risk helps you to think more deliberately and can be interesting for passengers. Example:

Home To Half Way To The Office—Distance One Mile

". . . the momentum from this burst of acceleration should carry us up the drive as far as the gate so that we reach it at barely rolling speed. I do this to allow time to watch for kids running on the grass verge outside our fence because only when I know this first danger is clear, dare I move the car out to the edge of the road. Then I always look right first because even up our quiet hill cars come fast and close to the grass.

"Now I'm gathering clutch control and keeping one hand at the ready on the choke as I look and double-check right and left. With a cold engine that's vital to prevent stalling half way out. All clear! So, off we go and I'm making an immediate check in the mirror as we straighten up. Wow! here's a fastard behind already. I'm moving in to let him pass and keeping a special eye on the Browns' gateway as I am not usually this close.

"Towards the bottom of the hill I shall use 2nd gear for engine braking keeping me well in control for our left turn into the road that crosses. There's a new fastard in the mirror now so I'm giving him extra brake light flashes to warn him we may have to stop at the bottom. He's "pushing" me already and this makes me doubt if he realises how fast drivers swish from the right at the T-join.

"Good, we're clear and he's lucky too. On this narrow bit while nothing comes the other way I am keeping well to the middle and watching all the driveways because people reverse out—especially being the school run hour. At the top T where the road crosses and we turn right to go down the hill I have to take a waiting position well to the left despite the fact that I am turning right because our road is so bottle-necked. If you don't you make it impossible for people to turn into this road—and it's usually your best friend's wife coming back from the station just down the hill who gets caught! There's another catch at this turn caused by this silly fence on the left that masks our view of anyone coming, especially on the pavement. I do the same "roll stop" technique here (as at my gate) because you quite often get some late blighter who's running down to catch the train, dive right across the bonnet. I suppose if you didn't know the area at least the tell-tale pavement edge would give you some clue! You have to show sympathy . . . and care.

"You can see further to the right here than you can to the left so I always look left last before and as we pull out. Right, it's clear, off we go! Mirror check. Nothing there. That fellow behind's had to wait because of this van coming up the hill. 2nd, 3rd, this is fast enough. I'm covering the brake already in case that chap waiting in the side road to the left hasn't seen us yet. He's not looking our way. I'm slowing the car instinctively—watching for swerving options—there's still no-one behind—hoot to warn—goodness! Stop! Would you believe anyone could pull out like that?

"Now we go on over this bridge and take left at the crossroads. I started to assess the crossroads immediately I reached the top of the bridge, as they came into view. You can see from there what's coming from the right and if there's anyone from straight ahead, or if it's clear, as it is this morning. This helps you get time when you reach it to watch the hidden latch gate on the corner on our left. You can just see it now. I swing fairly wide of it if I can, like today, because some young children live there.

17

"Now this S bend we are coming to needs care because there is a long straight at its far end and approaching drivers might misjudge their speed while entering it. It looks slightly damp on the first bit of the bend so I'm keeping her slow, not accelerating at all. Notice how I'm hugging my own side. There won't be much time if someone comes skidding towards me this wet morning!

"No marks for hard acceleration on this straight while the engine is still cold so I take it easy. 3rd gear as we pass this trunk road sign normally slows me just right for stopping when, we reach the main road.

"Turning left here it is essential to look left *last*—before moving! What happens is you drive up and stop as we are now and look right. Say that it is clear. So you look left. A steady stream is on its way into town but, you think, they need not affect my left turn. So you look right. Still clear, say. Do you go? . . . No Sir! because while you are sitting here waiting you can bet your life a fastard will pop out of the stream from the left and start overtaking the others. One move from you and you're dead!

"So, it's clear right and I'm looking left last. Today seems to be the exception—they're all behaving and we can go. I'm accelerating briskly because traffic catches up behind so fast if you dawdle. I keep a finger ready on the headlight flasher all the way along here because this road has a peculiar width which seems to encourage people to try and "force" a deadly third middle lane and there isn't room. There's one poking out from behind that lorry. Ah! he's accepted my warning.

"I'm easing off for the crossroads coming up despite give way markings against crossing traffic—covering the brake too. I find that pays, especially in rush hour when people waiting get more impatient . . ."

THINK WITH THE "OTHER" DRIVER

Consideration for others is the essence of good driving manners. Each road "reading" can have different implications for a lorry driver, a sports car man, a pedestrian or a mother with her baby buggy. The gap that is a headache for a ten-tonner is "chicken-feed" for a cyclist but a steep hill which buckles the cyclist's knees will be whizzed up by the empty truck. One needs to link consciousness of others' problems with thought.

Once your habit includes considering his or her view-

18

point it becomes natural to help, moving over, closing up, stopping or as appropriate whenever you can. The more of us that do so the more pleasure our roads will provide in the future.

THE HEAVY LORRY DRIVER

I recently had the pleasure and honour of working and driving with "big lorry" boys and specially thank my friends John Wales, Gordon, Tom, Gerry, Terry and Les, all of Express Deliveries, London, N.17. I hope that I gained some insight of how you can "think with" the lorry driver.

Their Pet Hates

1) Idiot parking near narrow street ends, depot entrances or other turn-ins which prevent them getting round.

2) Overtakers who immediately slow down. On a heavily loaded wagon with six or eight gears and a heavy clutch, being forced unnecessarily to go down and up the gearbox is good reason to be furious! It's more exercise than most people take in a week! Allow heavy vehicles to maintain speed and forego priority rights where you can make way for them. You case it for them and all behind them.

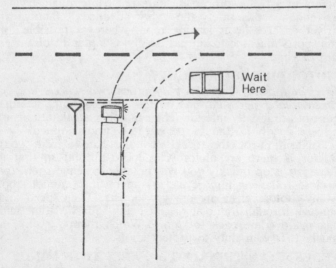

Fig. 1. Waiting well back for a lorry to emerge.

19

3) Drivers following who see the lorry's difficulty in entering a narrow street but still close up leaving them no reversing space. Don't or you may get squashed!

If a "big" boy is pulling from a narrow street into your road, also of narrow width, his rear wheels will have to cut the corner. Position well back (Fig. 1) to ease his task.

How To Help Them

1) Hoot when you overtake, when near enough to penetrate cab noises. Sports cars especially are not easily seen from high cabs.

2) You may see a "big" boy reversing unaided about to touch something hidden from his mirror; give rapid or long hoots to denote anguish and to alert.

3) Lorry drivers, when they overtake you, appreciate a headlight flash telling when it is safe to come in. With 60 feet bodywork this is hard to judge and there may be some danger ahead of the lorry which you cannot see compelling him to get in as quickly as possible.

"THINK WITH" THE SPORTS CAR DRIVERS

Well balanced powerful sports cars may reach 70 m.p.h. in less than half the time of a family saloon. Driven rightly, such cars overtake safely on short clear stretches while others in a traffic procession dare not contemplate trying. To enhance this safety the "very advanced" family car driver ensures he is leaving room wherever possible for the sports machine to zip past safely. Chapter 11 discusses fast driving.

MOTORBIKE OR MORGUE?

In Britain your chances of dying on two wheels are 18 times greater per mile than on four. Braking and steering control are greatly inferior. Their massive acceleration can also be deadly for the inexperienced or undisciplined.

Realisation of these facts counts. Know from your mirror if there are motorcycles loose around so that if forced to stop quickly you will be able to leave room for a close following motorcycle to slip by if it cannot stop. Many motorcyclists are crazy optimists. They speed and squeeze through traffic at risk of being squashed time and again and come back for more. Watch them . . . like a hawk. It is your duty to protect idiots.

PEDESTRIAN THINKING . . . KEEP IT IN MIND!

People dash out to get to the shops before they close.

In downpours they bolt for shelter. When traffic is particularly heavy they sometimes just get fed up waiting and walk straight out in front of you as anger takes over. In arctic weather pavements often remain icier than roads. People then prefer to walk *on the road*, dodging around parked vehicles. Expect them, especially in darkness and when roads have been cleared before pavements.

Blind Walkers

Take trouble to help the blind. If it is safe all round where they wait to cross and you are stopping, a touch on the horn may be used as a signal or you may be able to call through your window. (However 2 red reflective bands on the white stick mean the person is deaf too.)

Deaf Walkers

As, apart from above, you cannot distinguish them treat everyone on the basis that they might be deaf.

Old Walkers

Older people often lose their judgement of stopping distances although they try to be careful. It is simple courtesy to allow them plenty of time and not to frighten them as their pace is slow. Watch out for the special breed, mainly older men, who treat the road as their property. They cross slowly and smirk as though pleased to trouble you. Maybe they are bitter about the world but you could run them over if you are not aware of this mentality.

Young Children

Nowadays fortunately most children have learned to regard traffic seriously by six to nine years old but the very young ones still act on a whim.

Particularly near suburban schools where parked cars line the streets be watchful. Tea times and early morning are worst. If you killed someone's child as a direct result of blank-brained speeding you would have it on your conscience for life. Fig. 2 shows a potential example I witnessed.

A wee girl was standing beside the road holding her father's hand as I approached, following behind a delivery van. Concealed from the van driver and myself was her prized doggy. It was still hidden behind the parked car while we were coming along. The kiddy spotted her dog

21

Fig. 2. A near miss discussed in the text.

(arrowed) and without warning, wrenched herself free and dashed across towards it. Only a breathtaking lightning reaction by the van driver saved her.

The point holds true so often. You cannot assume anything where little children are concerned. The kiddy holding daddy's hand would have fooled 99 out of 100 drivers, including probably myself.

"THINK WITH" "RUSH-HOUR-ITIS"
Carelessness creeps in if travelling the same route daily. Speeds rise, over-confidence flourishes, rules are broken. Junctions are approached too quickly hoping to whip out smartly. Or the opposite, where you become sleepy, inattentive and slow, relying on knowledge from previous experience. Non rush-hour examples are postal vans, milk wagons and child cyclists.

Early birds may even have been confronted by one of these "automatic" drivers approaching actually asleep; my advice is to hoot in a series of "beep, beeps", flash headlights on and off, watch his front wheels and slow. By watching his wheels, you may be able to swing clear as a last resort.

PEAK DANGER PERIODS
Statistics show late Saturday nights to be the most dangerous on the road and worse if wet. This is when the

22

"idiot" hordes are out in force. Extra care is needed around pub closing times. The message: know the time, think where you are and be prepared. Become a *very advanced* thinker.

2

CAR CONTROL

SLOUCHED BODY—SLOUCHED MIND

Correct posture aids our sensory system to sound warnings in the brain. Unless stifled by a sloppy position, balance and listening devices in the ear and nerve messages from all over the body combine to provide essential, integrated information. Steering or braking mechanical faults, changes of road surface, punctures, and—vitally important—the beginning of skids—are examples which the sensory detective squad may signal.

This is so important I will go into detail. Look at Fig. 3. Press your bottom backward, arch your shoulders well back and you will discover the most relaxed yet alert position. The head held high and attentive, you properly command the view near the bonnet that may, in emergency, avert peril.

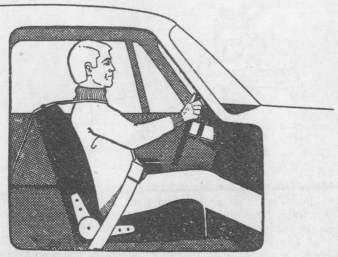

Fig. 3. Correct way to sit.

Arms Bent Or Straight?

You need to be able to work the pedals and gears positively, without stretching forward. Your leg should still be slightly bent when the brake is pressed hard. (In sports cars, although the legs are more horizontal, the same applies.)

You achieve maximum sensitivity, leverage and reaction speed in the arms and hands when the inside elbow angle is about 105°–130°. Fully stretched arms are tiring. On the other hand if you steer tucking your elbows close to your chest, you reduce leverage and induce tension. Aim to achieve as near the ideal position described as you can. Be certain the seat is secure after adjustment or the seat could shoot back and make your brake push ineffective—deadly danger.

Holding The Wheel

Fig. 4 a) shows the sensitive palm area, resting on the outside wheel rim. The fingers then wrap round the underside and thumbs point towards 12 o'clock along the top side as in Fig. 4 b). Whether a "nine-fifteen" position is better than one at "ten-to-two" o'clock is doubtful : variation around these positions matters not and is restful but both hands should remain above the horizontal centre line, except for turning.

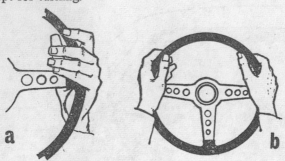

Fig. 4. Hand hold on the wheel.

Many Drivers Were Never "Taught" How To Steer

Unless we analyse how we steer it is usually done instinctively (and not too badly!). Here are my observations on the subject to compare with your own.

a) The built-in "self-centre" in most steering normally keeps the car straight. Conscious steering creates weaving!

You hold the wheel gently, as you would an egg. making the required corrections rather than constant "directions". After small steering movements allow self-centering to operate, lightly controlling the wheel as it returns (no jerks).

On uneven roads the bumps tend to turn the steering. Except on a severe bump the "self-centering" action of the steering will put the car straight again automatically—if you let it. Here you hold the steering wheel more firmly but allow it to turn slightly and correct itself as the bumps are encountered. The car will ride straighter than if you "fight" to keep the wheel straight all the time.

b) You never cross your hands. To turn substantially two movements are repeated alternately:

1) The hand next to the turning side pulls down while the other loosens grip to slide down and round the wheel so both arrive at the same time near the bottom —ready for movement two.

2) The slipped hand tightens its grip and pushes up, the other relaxing grip sufficiently to glide back ready to repeat (1).

3) Unless it has power assistance you should never turn the wheel of a stationary car. This induces wear; wait until the car is just beginning to move.

STARTING TIPS

Using the starter is the biggest drain that the battery has. You can lighten the load and prolong battery life by:

a) Switching off all the electrics—particularly the wipers and the lights but do not forget the electric rear window heater, the demister fan and odds and ends like the interior light; also turn the radio off. Even one such item can be critical if the battery is already extremely low.

b) Depressing the clutch when starting (otherwise some of the shafts in the gearbox are being turned with unnecessary waste of effort).

c) Never using more than brief bursts of starter and always allowing 30-second rest intervals in between each burst.

The secret of getting a naughty little bad starter to go is to panic *before* you have flogged the battery to death. A push, a tow, or the handle may be useless once you have extinguished every glimmer of life from the poor old battery so the thing to do is to try them *first* while you still have *some* juice. There is a state of charge at which the battery will still turn the engine feebly but at which there is no danger of the engine starting because the starter motor is taking all the juice, and none is getting to the sparking plugs. This is the stage where, if you stop caning the battery with the starter motor and you push the car instead, with luck you will be able to get her going.

When starting from cold you may find the following ideas are helpful:

1) If there is an automatic choke the book of words with the car will tell you the proper drill. Usually it is essential not to waggle your toe on the accelerator except perhaps in a specified way because this floods the engine.

2) With a manual choke, for the first burst of starter use choke only, no accelerator, being ready to catch it if it starts, with partial accelerator.

3) The second burst should then be as for the first.

4) If a third burst is needed use three-quarter accelerator but push the choke back off. Be ready to "catch" it this time with the choke, at the same time releasing most of the accelerator. (On certain cars with accelerator pumps also avoid agitating the accelerator unnecessarily or neat fuel will be squirted in, flooding the engine.)

5) Repeat four.

6) Go back and repeat two, three, four and five in order.

When all this fails check:

a) Ignition is switching on properly.

b) Anti-theft device.

c) Petrol. (Gauge may be faulty.)

If the car does not start within a dozen tries but the battery still sounds lively then it is time to become mechanically minded. Look at the battery terminals to see that they are both clean and tight. Check for firm, dry attachment at both ends of every plug lead and on all the leads to the coil. Further diagnosis requires skilled assistance but nearly always makes a lot more sense than futile battery bashing. The alternative solution would be jump leads.

Choke Tips

A finger held on a manual choke knob while in use prevents forgetting to put it back. The "fast" tickover is your double safety reminder, if you have left choke on.

HANDBRAKE TIPS

Apart from "fly-off" handbrakes, avoid the click, click, click of the ratchet by using the ratchet release; it saves wear.

Outside my office where there is a "pull in" for cigarettes, etc., parked cars regularly "run away". Because the ground looks flat, any half-hearted grab at the handbrake seems to do for many people in a rush. They do not think of leaving a gear engaged (or selecting P—automatic) to give the double safety of engine compression hold. It is astonishing how often this really does happen through slovenly habits of drivers involved.

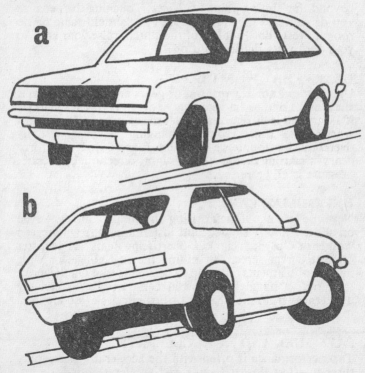

Fig. 5. Hill parking.
The front wheels are "chocked" almost touching the kerb:- a) facing downhill, b) pointing uphill.

Fig. 5 shows extra safe hill parking with the front wheels "chocked", almost touching the kerb, but not pressing on it (to avoid tyre damage). You shouldn't bang the wheel against the kerb during parking or steering as tyre damage may result. If you park facing up a hill which has no kerb to "chock" against leave the steering turned so that should the car move the back will run into the edge, not out. Always remember to lock the doors not only to safeguard against the risk of theft but for the safety of inquisitive children who might tamper with the brake.

USING THE CLUTCH

Pressing the clutch fully downward is unnecessary; just beyond the "biting point" suffices. Touching the pedal as you drive wears the clutch rapidly so, should there be no room to rest your foot left of the clutch, raise your knee so your foot rests flat in front of it.

GEARS THAT WON'T GO IN

Unless the clutch is worn out or gears are damaged then if she won't go in to 1st gear, move off in 2nd. On the move if 1st to 2nd is difficult, skip to 3rd, or if 2nd to 3rd won't work, take top. Trouble changing down is usually overcome by double de-clutching (page 30). Never force gears in causing damage; fingerlight, directionally precise, pressure is all you need.

UNFAMILIAR CAR

Never be lazy about memorising unfamiliar controls – even on short trips. A split-second lost finding the windscreen washer or dipswitch can kill. Sacrificing items like demister or heated rear screen, or noting the fuel guage, or wing mirror adjustments, adds up to accidents too. On the move look out; a harsh brake pedal can surprise, as can big differences from the steering or turning circle you are used to!

SAVE FUEL AND ... ACCELERATE

Top performance is often with the accelerator pedal only three-quarters down! Even rapid acceleration is little improved by using the last quarter. "Flat out" driving does not need the foot right on the floor; at medium speed you can slack off the pedal a surprising amount without losing speed. It is well worth reminding yourself from time to time if you want to save fuel.

Are You In The Right Gear, Dear?

Fig. 6 graphs peak engine acceleration power for an average saloon. Fastest, most economical acceleration keeps inside the power range in all gears. A speed outside this range in any gear wastes fuel and loses time.

A 5th gear is not shown because these are normally intended for saving fuel at cruising speeds, rather than for acceleration up thereto. Although you can pick up extra speed whilst in 5th, doing so will be sluggish and fuel-inefficient.

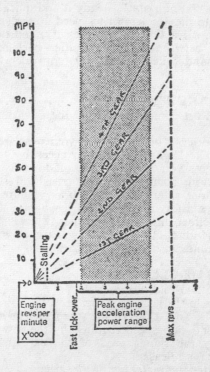

Fig. 6. Peak engine power.

THE UPHILL START JOKE

Even fairly advanced motorists may benefit from the following explanation. Provided engine revs are held sufficiently high to move the car forward up the hill, there is one point of release at which the clutch pedal can be held which stops the car rolling back downhill (handbrake off), but at which the gear is insufficiently engaged (because the clutch is not fully released), to move the car uphill. You are suspended between going up and rolling back. To start expertly uphill, bring the clutch to this "biting point" and hold it there; then let the handbrake off calmly and slightly add acceleration as you steadily release the remaining clutch.

Save time at slightly uphill brief stops by holding her on the footbrake. To go, take first, bring the clutch to just before the "biting point", steady it and quickly switch the right foot to the accelerator to speed up the engine. Adjust that clutch a fraction up (if necessary) and there you are, suspended between going and rolling back as if you had used the handbrake—a little deft footwork which is easily learned.

FOOTBRAKE TECHNIQUE

Braking effort comes more from the thigh than the ankle muscles.

To smooth out braking adjust your push from the thigh. If you brake slightly more than necessary to begin with this will give you room to ease off towards the end and allow a more comfortable jerk free "roll stop". Earlier and therefore safer warning of brake failure or a skiddy surface is a safety bonus of this technique. You se..se the retarding effect through your hands, by balance in the ear and by the amount of strength you use in your arms and legs to counteract being thrown forward.

DOUBLE DE-CLUTCHING

This has a two-fold purpose:
1) To help the gear cogs engage.
2) To pre-adjust the engine speed so that it matches the transmission speed required by the new gear for virtually the same speed of the car—just before the clutch is released.

The better the matching of the speeds in 2) the less jerk will be felt by passengers as the new gear becomes engaged.

With synchromesh gearboxes the need for 1) above has diminished. For this reason a half-way stage towards a double de-clutch has become a popular technique and I describe it first. It is only necessary for downward changes.

1) Depress clutch, at the same time releasing the accelerator (left foot down—right foot up).
2) Select next gear down without delay.
3) "Blip" the accelerator. Quickly release the clutch, timing the moment the gear will "bite" into engagement to coincide with the peak revs of your blip on the accelerator, or well before they have died away. Just how big a "blip" to give for a particular speed and when precisely to release the clutch comes with practice.

A full double de-clutch is slightly more complicated but it is sometimes the only means of changing gear without a crunch on a classic or thoroughbred car, built before the days of synchromesh. The method is as follows and the principle of matching the engine speed is the same:

The movements are carried out as quickly in succession as possible:

1) Clutch down—release accelerator, at the same time.
2) Slip gear to neutral.
3) Release clutch, fully.
4) "Blip" accelerator.
5) Clutch down fast, select next gear down, release clutch at once—while the extra engine revs last.

With a minimum of practice all these moves can be completed at lightning speed, although it looks a long job on paper.

On the historic car there may also be a need to double de-clutch when changing *up* the gears. The method is 1) as above, 2) and 3) as above, leave out 4); then 5) after a brief pause clutch down, engage the next gear up and release—then re-accelerate as you would after a normal gear change (if required). The moves are the same except you do without the accelerator "blip".

HEEL AND TOE GEAR CHANGING

This technique could equally be called heel and toe braking. Its purpose is to enable you to drop down the gears during braking so that when the need for slowing has passed you are already geared for maximum re-acceleration. The lower gears also help the brakes and give a more

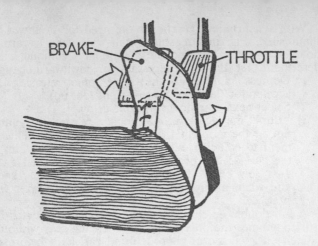

Fig. 7. Heel and toe.

controlled stop. If you have mastered the double de-clutch or have perfected the half-way stage to the DDC which was described first, you can combine either method with the heel and toe principle.

Fig. 7 shows how the heel of your shoe, or just the right side of the sole can be used to blip the accelerator pedal while the ball of the foot still keeps continuous braking pressure. This feels strange to begin with but with practice it becomes possible to maintain any level of braking pressure evenly, despite blipping the accelerator as much as you wish! If trying this for the first time choose moments when there is no traffic around you. And when you haven't *got* to stop!

SWITCHING OFF WINKERS AUTOMATICALLY
Make a habit of lightly touching the control arm with one finger whenever you straighten up the steering wheel after a turn. The habit is no harder to make than the one which tells you to signal in the first place!

BLINDING INTENSITY REAR FOG LAMPS
Excellent in fog or heavy snowing, these lamps all too often merely sting following drivers' eyes when switched on inadvertently at night or during a downpour.

TOM TOPPER'S "FIST FIVE" ROUTINE

One way to alert a driver that he is dazzling everyone behind, or – which is often more dangerous – that his winker is still on when he has finished with it, or – perhaps equally annoying at night – that his headlights are playing full beam into your mirrors, is by an unofficial signal I have dubbed Tom Topper's "Fist Five" routine. *Never to be used in an "I told you so." fashion,* it is only suggested as a means to inform another motorist of a light which may be dangerous that he may be unaware he has on. *One sign* to denote all such lights forgetfulness has, I hope, a chance of spreading to become a universal life-saving custom. Here's the drill: when comfortably ahead of the vehicle with the erring light, raise your left hand up between the headrests so that it is visible to the other driver. Alternately clench your fist and open your five fingers wide for a few moments, roughly at winker speed.

3

TOWN TECHNIQUE

MAIN ROADS IN THE TOWN

Important "through" roads and "ring" routes mostly have at least two lanes each way. Sometimes opposing traffic is separated only by bollards placed at regular intervals; sometimes there are stretches of fully equipped dual carriageway. Single line two-way conditions are encountered from time to time where there hasn't been room to build the road wider. I shall first discuss these main highways.

In driving, if a general philosophy can be established, a lot of difficulties can be removed. Reading this book will, I hope, help develop sound methods as you absorb, reject or improve the principles I have found most useful.

KEEPING TO THE RIGHT HAND LANE WHEN THERE IS MORE THAN ONE .

Normally where there are two or more lanes each way the right one is quicker and safer to use, even allowing for speed limits, because of three facts. 1) You have a reduced accident risk from side turnings and openings and from pedestrians or children stepping off the pavement. 2) You have no problems with parked cars. Inner lane vehicles often have to pull out to pass parked cars and by custom find they first have to give way to any vehicles overtaking themselves. The fear that some idiot may open his car

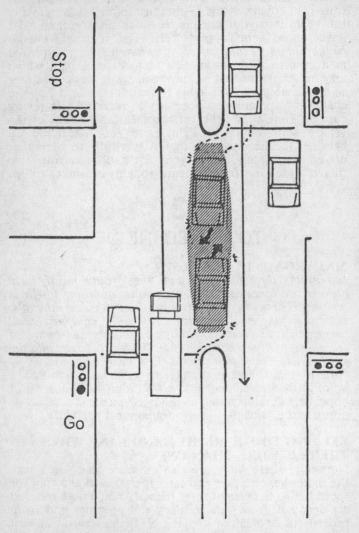

Fig. 8 (a). Keeping out of people's way when turning at lights.

door in your path is also removed. 3) You join the ranks of other, thinking, advanced right lane professionals, by-passing and keeping out ot the way of those of the inner

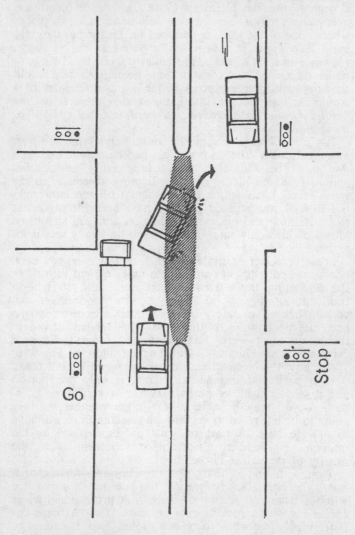

Fig. 8 (b). Baulking "straight ahead" traffic by bad positioning.

lane dawdling mentality. On average you have an easier ride in the right hand lane.

My right lane philosophy may seem to cross swords to a degree with the Highway Code's insistence on always eventually moving back to the left hand lane. In places where none of the reasons adduced for keeping in the right hand lane apply, a return to the left lane makes sense. However in a lot of areas, particularly the urban type ones under discussion, the constant lane changing which would tend to result is unrealistic. A better Highway Code attitude would include the proviso that *provided there is no one behind hoping to overtake you need not feel obliged to move in.*

It's not all sunshine in the right hand lane however. People ahead waiting to turn right can baulk you and then you must be adaptable. Good long range anticipation should give you plenty of time to move discreetly to the inner lane. A car which fails to signal till too late ought not to fool you because you will have seen his vagueness in positioning and his speed reduction and you should be ahead of his act, whatever it is, when he finally gets it together.

Sometimes, for example at lights, one or even two cars, positioned correctly in readiness to make a right turn when the oncoming traffic clears, need not baulk straight-on traffic at all. Fig. 8 (a) shows how a good driver can cocoon himself in safety in the shaded area provided he gets his car parallel to the road once he has driven in there. He as it were "manufactures" room for people originally behind him to flow through straight on. Fig. 8 (b) shows how the inconsiderate block everyone behind them.

In a particular instance therefore, if only one person ahead signals right, or perhaps two at a very large intersection, you may be able to pre-judge whether you are going to be left room to go through straight on or will have to change lane. A part of your judgement will be the opinion you have reached during following as to the quality of the driver in question!

There is bound to be the odd time however when changing to the inside lane before it is too late proves impossible without risking ill feeling or danger. A professional never forces his way across or cuts in; rather does he ease imperceptibly over when there is a "long" gap. It causes no harm to a driver if you occupy a sensible gap ahead of him when you are travelling at his speed. What is inexcusable is to squeeze in so that he has to slow up. You must be patient for a fair gap. In law too, you must wait. Watch out for that naughty motorcyclist in your mirror blind spot who chooses to shoot through on your left just as you pull over.

If you have moved to or were in the inner lane because of someone turning right you are provided with an instant safe way to regain the right hand lane at once as you pass him. See Fig. 9. It is almost certain nothing could be over-

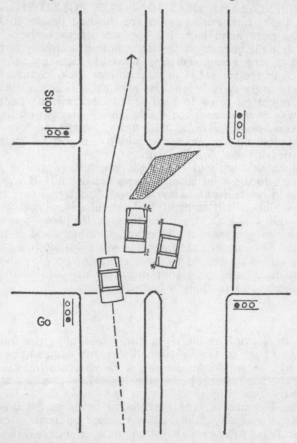

Fig. 9. Regaining the right hand lane.

taking you at this stage except a weaving motorcyclist (or it would hit the guy turning right) so all you need to be on guard for is traffic from the other direction right turning across you out of the area shaded in Fig. 9. (Note that they may be concealed from you till the last second by the vehicle you are getting round.)

Now I have outlined the mental approach to right lane driving here is a tip with which you can help drivers behind who have a similar philosophy.

HELPING LANE DECISIONS FOR FOLLOWERS

The lights turn red and you are the first person to stop in the right hand lane. No one was immediately behind you but the stream on the inner lane has already formed quite a long queue. Perhaps a minute ticks by and you notice in the far range in your mirror a car coming cautiously in the outside lane. He is clearly uncertain whether you might be going to turn right and is already nudging his way over towards the inside lane. A straight on signal, as you would give a policeman, which he can see silhouetted through your rear window, is just the message he's praying for! See Fig. 10.

When you wish to turn right yourself, please be considerate to the right lanesters who are behind! If you are going to be the front man waiting to turn, signal very early and maintain it if stopped, at least till several are behind you and winking. This gives those a long way behind a chance to anticipate the blockage accurately and in time. Should you cancel your indicator while waiting (once they have pulled up behind this is a relief for people's eyes at night or in rain) hold your finger on the control arm to remind you to re-apply it before going.

* * *

A final word on the right lane philosophy: one has no right to cling to the right lane if anyone wishes to pass—indeed this would be causing a moving obstruction, an offence (see page 88). As soon as safely possible, move in to let them through.

The increase of lane obstruction amongst the flowing traffic of our city suburbs has reached epidemic proportions. It is probably the most common offence and the one about which the police are doing the least. Because of it,

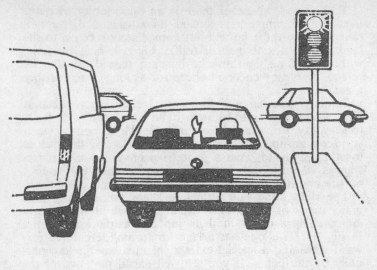

Fig. 10. Silhouetted signal for drivers behind.

another "crime", passing on the inside, has grown so commonplace that I am sure a lot of drivers mistakenly regard it as normal! The popularity of the first offence is reinforced for fear of complying and colliding with somebody trying a dodgy inside pass!

While the rules seem to count for nothing and our drivers continue lawlessly a gentle chide of our excellent police, who spend so much of their time catching people for easy things to prove like safe speeding (as opposed to unsafe speeding), is surely in order. No doubt it is more difficult to bring a prosecution for either of the above two examples of bad driving but until the driving public become aware that people are being successfully prosecuted these bad habits will proliferate.

TACTICS FOR KEEPING A CLEAR SPACE AHEAD OF YOU—ANOTHER DRIVING PHILOSOPHY

The professional likes the road immediately ahead uncluttered by Buppies. (Buppies were explained in chapter 1.) Having a clear stretch in front is a safer proposition than jogging along in the middle or at the back of a stream. You can see the problems that lie ahead to the fullest advantage. You have room to manœuvre.

To this end whenever there is an opportunity to move ahead of an immediate stream an advanced driver will take it. Once there he will not immediately race on to the back of the next bunch of traffic, but will bide his time, without holding up those he has just passed, so that he retains his clear "cocoon" ahead for as long as reasonably possible.

Similarly another way to ensure a clear space ahead is if a chance occurs to allow a build up of traffic in front to get away. For example you may be able to pull up when you see a group of people at the kerb collecting themselves together ready to cross a pedestrian crossing—in circumstances where strictly speaking, because none had a foot on the crossing itself, you need not have done so.

The right hand lane principle keeps you moving past many snarls of traffic. Here are a few more hints. You are approaching a red traffic light junction as the artist shows in Fig. 11. This one has a lane for turning left, three forward lanes and a special extra right turn lane, held separately by the lights. If you see well ahead that two of the forward lanes have filled up with traffic waiting for green it makes sense to choose the third free lane early and use careful timing so that you arrive in the front row as green

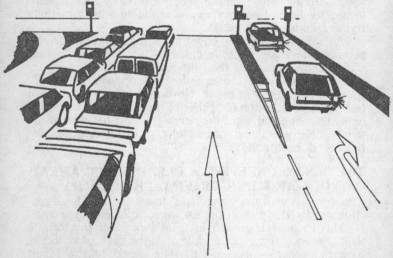

Fig. 11. Choosing the empty lane.

appears. You must beware of pedestrians straying across and of maniacs shooting red crossing your bows but by this means you can sometimes "overtake" whole bunches of traffic safely as they begin to move off.

The expert by making use of space available on the road can often, without discourtesy, get far ahead of the inexperienced and his doing so *creates more room for the novice* – a bonus that some woodentops at the Department of Transport appear to prefer not to see. Since this book was first written these "armchair" drivers have dreamed up further rules in the Highway Code to caution you . . . "In a traffic hold-up, do not try to 'jump the queue' by cutting into another lane or by overtaking the vehicles waiting in front of you." . . . "When traffic is moving slowly in queues and vehicles in a lane on the right are moving more slowly than you are . . . you may move to a lane on your left only in order to turn left or to park. Do not change lanes to the left in order to overtake."

While much of the Code is not law, in practice much of the law supports it! No-one would argue with the laudable purpose of these rules of preventing drivers from swerving in and out indiscriminately and dangerously or cutting in front of each other but there really is no sense in the "blanket" nature of the wording which has been used. I doubt that any British judge would criticise a driver who made use in a hold-up of a spare lane or space which would otherwise have been wasted, so long as he had not done it by cutting across or taking "unfair" advantage or in some way which had been a genuine hindrance to another driver.

When you are waiting in front at lights there may be an opportunity to get clear of bunched vehicles. Over-enthusiasm for a "Grand Prix" start, however, invites death. Racing is illegal. Nevertheless a swift get away is usually advantageous because it takes you clear of the clutter of traffic. Take care because motorcyclists may have squeezed up close either side, and bollards or the pavement line ahead may be going to force you off course. It is odd how light jumpers operate more in fog, snow and on wet nights! Look out!

In getting off the mark quickly and building up to cruising speed there is no need to waste fuel or strain the engine if you make the best use of the power range of your engine shown by Fig. 6 and practise snappy gear changes which save seconds. A sloppy change loses valuable yards. Changing too early or too late slows you even more.

Many lights have green filter arrows on one lane. We all, occasionally, find ourselves in such a lane by mistake when the arrow comes up in green. It is a hallmark of the advanced driver that even if he has made a mistake, he will go in the direction of the arrow, knowing that he has no right to baulk correctly positioned people behind. White lane arrows are often painted on the road at lights and all too frequently they are ignored. For example, a right hand lane is frequently intended to be reserved for those turning right but is used for traffic going straight on as if the arrow on the road did not exist. Because traffic in the next door lane cannot predict such misuse of the arrowed lane it can be argued that such driving is careless. Equally there may be places where turning traffic gets stuck behind straight on traffic which is incorrectly positioned but having to wait. The advanced driver will always select his lane in such a way that no other traffic is held up irresponsibly.

Changing Lane When Opportunity Knocks

Imagine middle laning in thick traffic on a three lane urban dual carriageway, knowing that you will want to turn right at the next major junction. The turn you require need not yet be in sight when you notice that someone alongside or just behind in the outside lane starts to signal left. This is your chance to signal right, watch his reaction and, all being well, you will be able to scissor-swap gaps. Probably whichever of you was slightly ahead to start with will be the forward part of the scissors movement and vice-versa. Equally there may be a driver ahead indicating left and searching his mirror who provides your opportunity. Acting when opportunity knocks instead of at the last second before a turn, saves a hold-up for both lanes!

BUS LANES

Bus lanes are a theft of road space which is being paid for by all tax paying motorists; they represent a classic example of the sort of creeping discriminatory legislation motorists continually face. While snarled jams costing the country fortunes in wasted time and pollution fume helplessly alongside the 80% empty bus lanes, millions of £££'s worth of tarmac stay reserved in all but idleness for the sake of a marginal benefit to the bus passengers—a ludicrously small proportion of total road users. I love buses but favouritism can get unbalanced! The bus lanes also provide wonderful sport for the more frivolous type of policemen. Thankfully individual bus lanes normally have set times during which they operate. As an advanced motorist I hope that you will observe the signs and whenever legal make use of the bus lanes. Too many motorists are assuming that they are 24-hour lanes or not bothering to look, and hence clogging up the rest of the road even more than the insult of these lanes means they need to.

THE IMPORTANCE OF EYE RANGING

Eye ranging near and far ahead, each side, and mirror-wise close and far behind, all the time, is good exercise for eye muscles and is the key to knowing the changing requirements around you. You need an all round running picture constantly focussing in your mind.

Bringing Science To Sight

Hawk-eyed vision is developed rather than inborn and is methodical. As the scene unfolds in front of him the expert plans to look in the right direction at the right time so as to be free to concentrate on any supreme potential danger points as they are reached. Every opportunity of seeing behind trees, obstacles, parked vans (under these as well), through railings, round, beyond and underneath as well as *through* a car in front, and so on, has to be taken as it arises. Opportunities are often lost once you get closer. You must seize your chances for glances and thus create more time for decisions and for a second look at extra risk areas pin-pointed in advance, e.g. openings between parked cars, groups of apparently unaccompanied toddlers, etc.

The experienced, healthy, exercised eye continually casts everywhere while the brain acts on the information by continual adjustments of speed, position or whatever. The areas *between* what seem to be the obvious risk points are not dismissed. These are taken in and assessed during the safer moments and this way no time is lost. Within the scope of human concentration everything is covered. There may be only one safe moment when a particularly difficult hazard can be checked. The expert will check it at that moment.

The scope for vision may often be increased by re-positioning your car slightly to one side or the other. All-round running knowledge must confirm first that this is safe but in any case you must avoid weaving; and no zig-zagging! Adjustment of the gap ahead between you and the next car is another visual master card. It is a con-tinuing process of using wits to see "everything" every-where.

On nearing a potential danger point unseen accident risk is likely to be increasing rapidly. Speed must be controlled with discipline. Position may need to be altered to safety advantage—above all being consistently sure you maintain room to stop, or space into which to swerve safely. Be ready for the unexpected insofar as anyone can.

Preparatory Moves That Make "Danger" Safe

Nearing possible trouble, a finger rests at the horn ready for a toot that could prevent a crisis, the feet hover over brake and clutch to reduce the thinking time factor of stopping distance. Speed, in check anyway, is restricted to occasional dabs of acceleration at safer moments but the brake foot remains ever ready to bring you to a sudden stop if the possible emergency happens. Spaces for escape by swerving are constantly reviewed and taken into account.

In the desperate unpredictability of an unforeseeable emergency, "running knowledge"—which practically averts the need for further conscious thought—is essential if split-second alternatives to disaster are to be grasped before they slip away.

It is not enough to keep your eyes roving. The gaze must never dwell but should range widely, repeatedly. Circum-stances change like lightning as the child breaking from the father's grasp illustrated a few pages back. Be alert. Intelligent anticipation comes to those who keep on the ball.

Accident victims are often uncertain what happened, so perhaps I may be forgiven for reiterating the importance of constant attention and thought while driving, till it be-comes instinctive with experience.

Save the eye muscles by moving your neck! Let it flex freely. It also staves off the day when you must finally accept that you have arrived as a stiff-necked, accident-prone, geriatric motorist!

AND NOW THE MIRRORS

Correct use of the mirror enables positioning so that traffic behind always has plenty of advance warning of your intentions. This along with your signal deters them from trying to pass dangerously when you are about to turn or change lanes. Of greater importance is the running picture of the scene behind which is gained by consistent mirror attention. Foreknowledge of that scene may be an indispensable part of your armoury in an emergency. Mirror glancing skill while the road is safe ahead makes sure that it does not need to be a distraction if danger should arise. 95% to 98% concentration must be out in front so your 2% to 5% mirror time needs to be well used.

A good picture has to be obtained by quick glances, no more but sufficient to develop the picture of all that is behind and what is behind that and vaguely further behind. No need to know the shape of the girl driver, only that she is there, whether she is closing up, falling back or holding her position. Because motorcycles and even cars can remain masked in your mirror blind spots (see Fig. 12)—

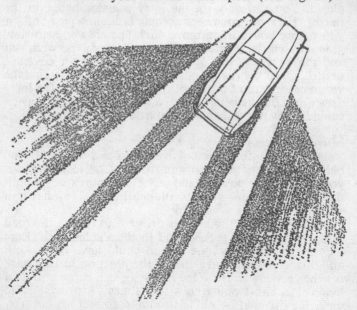

Fig. 12. Mirror blind spots.

especially if you are driving at a constant speed—only continuous attention to glances in the mirror will make sure that you pick them out.

With a lot of following traffic loose around it is sometimes wise before you move out to overtake, or in to change lanes etc., to confirm the exact proximity of what you know is behind or to the side, by a rapid glance over the shoulder during a safe moment. Many "L" teachers ignore this. The result is thousands of inflexible drivers who never take to an essential safety technique.

Are Mirrors Enough At Traffic Lights?

No. Motorcycles and cycles creep up while you wait. A look round before moving registers in your mind their existence and position—essential information even if you are not turning left or right.

Mirror Art

Imagine a lorry thundering close behind along a dual carriageway and you are preparing to overtake a slower car ahead. You can only see the lorry radiator badge in the mirror. How can you check nothing is zipping past both of you before you start to move out? The answer is to slow gradually a little, then accelerate to create a gap between you and the lorry enabling you to obtain the mirror coverage needed. Or, if the road bends, even a little, you may find the vision needed, most probably in the wing- mirror. The lorry driver may dislike being slowed down but it is fair to say he should know better than to breathe down your exhaust pipe.

Mirror Courtesy

The mirror informs you of overtakers and of what traffic behind is shortly going to want to do. Courtesy demands your help where possible and safe. You sometimes benefit many behind you whereas thoughtlessness, even for a second, can create a hold-up.

Fig. 13 shows a thoughtless driver who blocks the road instead of keeping parallel and in the shaded area. Bare inches over and everyone behind could have moved on, and this would also have opened the junction further back for the crossing traffic. One road-clog can cause a mile of trouble! A short polite hoot sometimes "instructs" such an erring driver if he still has room to correct his mistake. It is so selfish and happens so often.

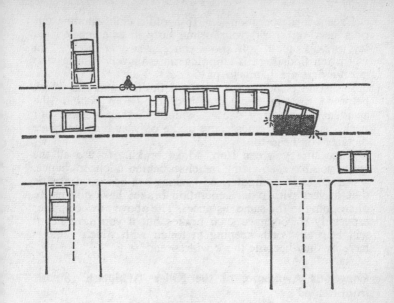

Fig. 13. A thoughtless driver or road-clog.

Moving in for overtakers, even if only a little, confirms to them that you know they are passing. This may be a vital reassurance, leaving them free to concentrate on every other factor potentially affecting the pass. When you are being passed it is not enough to merely feel involved. Beware, because you are committed, whether you like it or not, to the safety of everyone who could be at risk should *you* blunder through action or inaction.

Unfortunately, trained mirror users, except at turns, are almost non-existent in Great Britain. Good as the maxim "mirror, signal, manœuvre" may be it has overshadowed the proper advice "mirror, mirror, mirror". Reflect on it.

Lapse of Mirrors—"Running"—Knowledge

Even a good mirror user occasionally forgets and lands in trouble without knowing whether swerving might swipe a cyclist to his death. To swing to avert one disaster can create another. Swerving into an unseen passing car may push it through the Pearly Gates.

Except in desperation (e.g. to avoid a child running out or a head-on crash) your prime duty in emergency is to try to stop unless you *know* you can swerve safely. You will often find there is stopping time anyway. Those who swerve first are likely to pay, later!

A second principle for mirror defaulters and one which helps to prevent being smashed into from behind (the accident which may cause "whiplash", i.e. breaks your neck), is this: in emergency, brake only as hard as space dictates you need to.

Once sure you can stop, adjust braking to use all the space you have, so giving the chap behind a longer chance.

Advances in computerised braking are now so dramatic that drivers with older generation brakes have no chance of stopping in the same distances. The above advice applies especially if you have such brakes but if you have not it will be well worth keeping in touch with which vehicles have as they become more widespread!

Conscious Avoidance of the Killer "Whiplash" Smash from Behind

Brake lights warn followers . . . if they work! Your brake lights reflect on headlamps behind, so can be checked in your mirror while queueing, or, more positively, check them with a friend!

Flash them to alert followers in advance of probable stopping by lightly touching the brake pedal—a great safety technique where you are reasonably certain that people behind will not yet be able to see a possible danger far ahead which you can!

Emergencies apart, there should be no such thing as sudden stops but some people seem happy to create "emergencies"—for example lunatic drivers who stop three feet out in the road on a "clearway" while they look at their map. The fact that they have stopped often isn't noticed quickly enough by fast flowing traffic catching up behind. Suddenly one blissfully unaware idiot has put dozens of cars at risk. They usually do it just round a corner or over the brow of a hill too!

BRAKING AND TRAFFIC FLOW

Imagine two lanes of traffic going in each direction on a busy urban clearway. Traffic lights, pedestrian crossings, etc., force traffic to stop from time to time, but the general forward flow is swift.

You can plan your driving to help keep this flow going. The more of us who do the smoother we shall see traffic flowing:

1) After any stop, add speed swiftly, till you regain the flow speed.

2) Just as you should avoid the dawdle start, avoid the dawdle stop but no sudden stopping, which risks the rear end pile up both for you and others further behind.

Judge your stops so that your brake application has to be at about 25% of foot pressure when compared with the force you would apply for an emergency stop. Slowing more gradually is a good fault but the trouble is—from a traffic flow point of view—that the drivers behind you will tend to see your early brake lights as a loud warning. In turn they will slow more than you have. Not so very far behind you the line of cars can come to a stop while you are still moving, albeit slowly!

Then, because so few are nifty in picking up speed again, the flow is broken for the cars involved. You may not have had to stop before the reason for stopping removed itself but they will find themselves stopped after it has gone!

Had you left your braking till later; a) the reason for stopping could have cleared itself before you needed to brake. Traffic could then have continued uninterrupted; b) if a stop was still necessary, the whole line would have to stop anyway so no-one would lose.

3) Moving traffic frequently has to slow a little, perhaps while someone turns off, and then it picks up speed and flows on. Rather like stopping too gradually, if you slow more or earlier than necessary, drivers behind will too. And in turn the effect will be magnified as the reaction spreads along the line behind. So braking for slowing should also be judged, leaving it till application at about 25% of foot pressure is needed.

49

4) Always have in mind the turning off principle explained below.

Turning Off Principle
Part 1—Get off the main road quickly! (Where safe.)
Part 2—Where you can, position to permit following through traffic to flow on; use every inch of available safe space!

Turning quickly applies more to left turns than right, though if several are behind you ready to turn right, your quickness may provide opportunity for an extra car or two to follow safely. Except where the opening is blind or pedestrians prevent you, be snappy is the motto for left turns. Dawdling frustrates the stream following and may force them to brake, go down the gears, or even jam on—probably unnecessarily. Using space to the last inch must include "slip-offs"—from where they start! Many roads and modernised "through" routes are now designed so that a turning car can slip off the main carriageway up to 30 or 50 yards before the turn. The pavement is deliberately set back. Too many motorists do not make use of them, however a polite toot sometimes encourages people. An equally usable "slip on" is normal for those coming out of such turnings.

Reveal Indicators Ahead to Others Behind
Once someone ahead indicates, and if "running" mirror knowledge shows it is safe, re-position to enable the driver behind you to see the signal as well. Your sideways movement also confirms to the driver ahead, via his mirror, that you have accepted his signal. Move slightly right or left as required.

In the case of someone ahead about to make a turn, the alternative of bringing on your brake lights at once can result in people behind stopping, perhaps unnecessarily, when they could have been preparing to filter. Where the intention of the man in front is overtaking traffic further ahead, rather than turning, your movement confirms that you understand and will not begin to pass as he pulls out.

Re-positioning Calms Pedestrians
You may be going fast on a wide road when pedestrians start to cross too close for comfort. Rule 1 is ease your

50

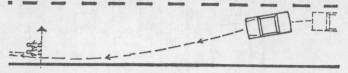

Fig. 14. The "steering" message.

foot on the accelerator and brake if necessary. But, where safe, give pedestrians the steering message. Then they know at once you will take care of them. The driver in Fig. 14 tells the walkers he has seen them by pointing his car temporarily behind them as well as braking. In many different circumstances "steering" messages can be given to help other motorists. It is a fundamental driving art to be developed.

NOSE TO TAIL
Fig. 15 shows a wide traffic light junction clogged with traffic, of which that turning left is at the most doing 12 to 15 m.p.h., a dangerous speed nevertheless.

Car A (Fig. 15) nose-to-tail behind one lorry has been hurried by amber appearing; the other lorry prevents moving to the inner lane. All three are turning left and keeping lane discipline but the right hand lorry masks an oncoming motorcyclist from Car A.

Nose-to-Tail "Grass Roots" Principle
The danger in this example is common to many situations and a cautious grass roots principle can easily save life.

Keep your whole car—including the right hand front corner of the bonnet as you go round—tucked within the space just used by the larger vehicle ahead. If you allow that corner of the bonnet even a fraction over that line as car A is going to in Fig. 15, you risk a crash with such a hidden motorbike. The rear right hand corner of the lorry prevents you seeing him till it is too late. I have put a star where the motorcyclist could collide with your wing.

The lorry must now be allowed to pull away well ahead

51

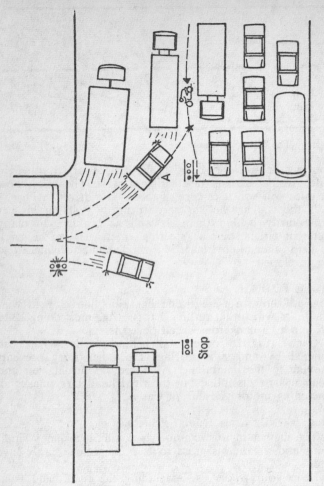

Fig. 15. Nose-to-tail.

before you ease out to see beyond it should you wish to.

Fig. 15 highlights another problem which is growing as traffic congestion in our cities ever increases. Sometimes traffic waiting, such as the motorcyclist was attempting to overtake in Fig. 15, stretches for a quarter of a mile or more. This sort of queue particularly tends to happen during the rush hours in the morning and evening. With more traffic closing up behind you and the lorry on your left you can, as driver of car A, find yourself severely hemmed into the outside lane as you all pick up speed. As the block of traffic of which you are part begins to hurtle along at ever-increasing speed risks multiply around you alarmingly. No matter whether you are hooted at from behind, or overtaken on the inside or whatever you simply *must ease back* in order to gain vision. There may be further motorcyclists coming down on the outside of the stopped traffic to your right; there may be jay-walkers coming out from behind stopped vans, etc., amongst it; crossing traffic may be nudging its way out through it, or some narrowing of the traffic lanes on your side, for example due to roadworks, may mean that whoever is on your left squeezes out on you (which he should not of course) robbing you of your road space. Where you can it makes sense to keep ahead or stay well behind such traffic snarls, especially where space is restricted and vision diminished.

For Turning Left An "Unofficial" Signal May Be Easier

If the road is otherwise clear it may be safe for a waiting car to pull out as you turn in. Your "steering" message by correct positioning and speed reduction confirms your indicator but a hand signal removes all doubt. The official signal is correct but Fig. 16 shows an "unofficial" one, easier to give (especially in wet weather). In different circumstances this extra signal confirms to those behind that you will be turning. Few people—quite rightly—trust indicators alone!

Fig. 16. Unofficial left signal for those behind.

Making Visual Safety When You Helpfully Stop For People

Fig. 1, page 19, shows stopping well back to ease the task for a lorry driver coming out who, due to his length, has to "cut" the corner. On a "through" route where drivers in two lanes have to stop, the "well back" principle is doubly important. What is also vital is the wide angle of vision the lorry driver, or any driver needs in order to see if any motorcycle is passing you. You prevent accidents by giving such a turning driver the chance to see for himself if it is safe.

Make Time While Green Lasts

Imagine you are going to turn right at some traffic lights a little way ahead and that they are showing green. The road you will enter has two lanes on your side. Approaching the lights from the opposite direction to you the road is empty except for one car and its driver commences a definite signal that he is going to turn left, into the same road as you are going to enter.

If you are extremely careful you may be able to save seconds by entering the road side by side, you into the outer lane, and he into the left hand one. What you do is to encourage him to turn neatly into the inner lane by nosing craftily forward as he approaches the turn. But don't commit yourself until you can see that he will co-operate. Any crash might be judged as your fault.

JOINING "THROUGH" ROUTES FROM SIDE ROADS AT "T" JUNCTIONS

Traffic sweeping along in double streams need not be so hard to join.

Turning Left, Joining A Main Road With Two Lanes Each Way

By taking a good forward position you are ready if it is safe to cut time by tucking into a gap in the left lane without having to wait for right lanesters to clear. Even if you require to cross to the outer lane almost at once (so as to leave the main road to the right) the task may become easier if you can use the left lane first as you would an acceleration lane.

As soon as you are in the left hand lane if that is the case, signal for moving to the right lane. Watching in your mirror and over the shoulder if need be, get over at the first safe gap so as to allow the drivers now behind you time to note you will soon turn right.

In joining an empty left lane while the right one is full a snag which is becoming more common is for one of those right lanesters to cut in left (towards you) as you pull out. Maybe he wants to turn left a little further on but more than likely he's suddenly decided to try a dodgy inside overtake. Watch for him!

Even in the seconds of turning (left or right) cars can arrive behind which were not in sight when you last looked. Develop a saving system: Make a habit to check the mirror as you straighten up. You thus come to associate straightening up with the mirror checking, and will always do it. You are automatically alerted if it is necessary to accelerate swiftly away from any arriving speedster, or to make room immediately for one to pass.

Turning Right, Joining A Main Road With One (or two) Lanes Each Way

At some "T" junctions unless you tackle them in two halves, blocking traffic from the right first, you may wait for hours. Vast care in selecting where this can be safely done is required. You cannot shoot out and risk an accident with fast traffic from your right but when it has ceased for a long space—and no one is about to turn right from the other direction into your road—may be your cue to move out and block the first half. Make sure fresh traffic from the right will see you in good time: the brow of a small hill might hide you from view, for example; remember what's safe in daylight may be daft in darkness.

Despite rude hooting as drivers have to pull up, they have no greater right to drive along the main road than you have to wait on it prior to turning right; that is, so long as you got there first when the road was clear. With two lanes your side the risk of being hit while waiting can sometimes be reduced by stopping at an angle so you only block the outer one.

Blocking should be carried out boldly *when safe*, or not at all. Never inch out. You may be tempted thinking crawling traffic will stop but, crawling or fast, people bash on and the danger is in trying to swing round you they crash with someone coming the other way—particularly into someone who, since your creepage, may have positioned to turn right down the road you are leaving. This is a favourite combination (comedy?) of errors in the night rush hour. When you are turning right off a main road be chary if you see potential "creeps".

Having taken the "blocking" position occupy it only for the minimum time necessary. If need be apply similar techniques to those explained above under the heading "turning left, joining a main road with two lanes each way".

While "blocking", if any car from your left begins to signal for turning right to where you have come from there may be time for you to accelerate briskly into the outer lane he will vacate whilst he is slowing up and positioning. (Traffic behind him will be filtering to his left or blocked). Watch out for zebra crossings or anything that could prevent you reaching your new stream speed quickly which, concentrating on your manoeuvre, you may otherwise fail to notice.

Crossing "Through" Routes

Similarly, blocking traffic on your right may be the one hope here. Then traffic from the left, seeing your situation, often stops and lets you over.

Once all the main road traffic has stopped, it is sensible for *all* the crossing traffic to be allowed over. Otherwise time is only lost for another bunch of main road traffic which will have to pull up. (Notice that if you are travelling on the main road and traffic in the other direction has pulled up in this sort of circumstance then, if you have the opportunity to do so, it is an occasion for advanced thoughtfulness for other drivers. The few seconds you may lose in stopping may be minutes gained for many times the number of drivers.)

If you are tailing across while a gap is available you should keep close but being wary as main road traffic creeps forward. Look out either way for mopeds queue-jumping blindly in these situations.

If there is "solid" traffic the advanced driver occasionally helps the progress of the crossing traffic by resorting to "doubling" as shown in Fig. 17. Much depends on the opening into the main road.

Normally at junctions of this kind drivers wishing to go

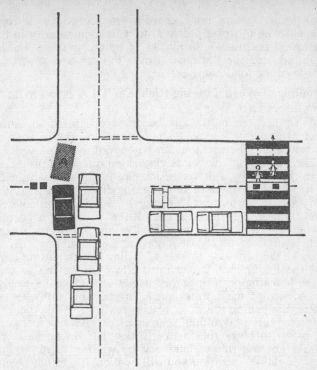

Fig. 17. "Doubling" (see text).

straight ahead wait near the centre line, leaving room for anyone going left to filter out. In "rush hour" conditions it is fast becoming customary for expert drivers to form a second straight on queue in this space. Then, as each driver in the normal queue edges out to block traffic from his right, the leading driver in the "second queue" moves out beside him—making use of the protection from traffic from the right that his blocking movement affords. The position recorded by Fig. 17 shows an expert in this "protected" position. He and the other front driver moved out to block the first half of the road while the lorry and stopped cars from the right were waiting the other side of the zebra as the walkers crossed.

The "expert" may now need to take the initiative in blocking traffic coming from the left when the first safe opportunity occurs but, according to the width of road available, he must be prepared to wait momentarily in the shadowed position A, in Fig. 17, if by trying to go first he might squeeze the "normal" driver too far over on to the offside of the road being entered.

"Doubling" When Turning Right On To A Road With Two Lanes Each Way

A similar technique has become recognised as more efficient at many T-joins. Some have arrows on the road to confirm this. The method can be cautiously employed.

The "doubling" driver, having eased out while protected from the right by a driver beside him in the normal queue, then moves forward to block traffic from the left at the first safe opportunity. (This may be possible immediately if no traffic comes from the left.) If the driver in the normal queue now makes his turn neatly into the outside lane there should be plenty of room for the "doubling" driver to make the turn side by side with him into the inside lane. But the "doubling" driver must allow for having to wait in the blocking position if there is not enough space, to give precedence to the normal queue driver (and any who tail efficiently behind him) to get away first. While waiting beforehand the "doubling" car should keep a few feet back so as not to block the first car's view left. In fairness you should not use this technique if by waiting to move into the "doubling" position you will be blocking traffic behind you which wishes to turn left. Only use it where the width is such that you are still leaving them room to get away left.

Chock-A-Block Through Route Bedlam

During rush hour the flow of traffic along many four-lane roads seems relentless. In suburban conurbations are found devilish junctions where much local "school" traffic has to cross this flow every morning and evening. To draw attention to the plight of this joining or crossing traffic in an attempt to make it safer, additional bollards have been placed in the middle to separate the two lanes of traffic in each direction on the through road. As well as the bollards hatch markings have been provided to try to reduce the through road traffic to one lane each way as it passes through the junction and create a safer no-man's-land in the middle of the junction. All this is fine when there are only one or two cars trying to cross or turn and main road traffic is sporadic. At rush hour, however, you may have half-a-dozen cars waiting either side of the main road, some wishing to turn right, some wishing to go straight across, some to turn left and in addition a number of the main road cars may be trying to turn right off the main road from each direction.

Despite being funnelled into single file the main road through traffic will often zoom on remorselessly for what seems an age without any decently safe gap appearing in it. Because it is travelling at 35 m.p.h. to 40 m.p.h. there is no chance of moving safely out to block it. To wait for more than 10 minutes is no longer rare. Even then you are often only able at first to try to get to the half-way no-man's land and hope to wait there if you cannot clear at once.

When your turn comes to be front marker in the side road, you must ignore the impatience which may be growing behind you, as you decide when to nip smartly forward to a safe waiting position if such be needed.

With the *shameful* speed that main road traffic keeps coming at these sort of junctions one dare not leave the side road unless the space in the middle to which you are moving is *guaranteed*, that is, no-one from right, left or centre is likely to drive on to it and sit there before you arrive thus leaving you stranded. That is a sure fire way to get hit!

Be ready for other drivers intending to use the "doubling" or "blocking" techniques discussed earlier in these pages as your eagle eye watches in every direction for anyone who might rob you of that space. To help you forecast what other drivers will do have in mind clearly who would have priority on the no-man's-land but remember that standing on your rights is pretty difficult when you are lying up in Mayday! (Generally, right turning main road traffic comes first, then straight across drivers would take precedence over those coming out of the side roads wanting to turn right. Take note in calculating where anyone may pull up to wait, whether the layout is conducive to any of the right turners trying to pass in front of each other. Unless established by road markings or custom, behind passing ranks more correct than the in front method.)

ZEBRA CROSSING SAFETY
Your brake lights warn followers as you stop. Watch that

any driver alongside you is also stopping, if not a hoot may alert him but the main point of it will be to alert the pedestrians. While an arm stopping signal tells pedestrians, the danger is that approaching drivers from the other direction may not see it. An advanced answer gaining favour is a prolonged headlight flash which is sure to alert a dreamy driver who then sees you stopping.

HEADLIGHT FLASHING

The Highway Code discourages headlight flashing other than in situations where you would hoot. Much of the Code is not law nor the beginning or end of road wisdom. Let us first consider them as an alernative to the horn.

1. If a driver hugs the centre of the road and you want to pass, you can often alert him from his sleep-driving, without noisy hooting, by a flash or two. Especially at night or in dull weather this catches his eyes in his mirror or screen and hopefully he will move in.

2. At night, at crossings, corners, etc., un-dipping and dipping form a silent substitute to the horn and used within reason are excellent safety aids. They are often more effective than the horn.

3. During *daylight* overtaking in busy areas, especially the "killer" three lane two way road, it is worth keeping headlights on (*plus* winker—to draw maximum attention to what you are doing) all the time. This informs everyone "I am coming through" but bear in mind there is less advantage on foggy murky days when the law dictates headlights all round anyway.

4. Certain roundabouts on trunk dual carriageways are chiefly built to slow up the trunk traffic in order to make it safe (partly via the "give way to your right" rule) for traffic from smaller roads to cross or join the dual carriageway, for example where there has been a black spot. Whereas on roundabouts which mark the intersection of several major routes, traffic from whatever direction tends to slow right down on entry, on the roundabouts we have described the tendency is for the trunk traffic scarcely to slow down for the roundabout. To be fair to these drivers they probably represent 98% of the traffic using the roundabout. It follows therefore that anyone doing other than skirting the roundabout along the dual carriageway liké they are, is in a distinct minority. Anyone who is going *round* to leave the dual carriageway to the right, or in order to go back up the

other way, or who is turning right or going straight across from a minor road, is going to meet fast right hand lane carriageway traffic arriving in on his left on his way round. This fast entry traffic should give way to him; the trouble is they frequently do not spot him, for example, peeling out of the dual carriageway traffic in the other direction in order to come round. In daylight you can increase your chances of being spotted as odd one out by having your *headlights on* as you come round into conflict with this fast incoming traffic. You will find your headlights stand out brilliantly where your indicator alone might not have been enough, although on dark days, as in 3 above, this advantage is reduced.

Headlight Flashing Customs

Despite the Code customary and courteous uses of headlight flashing have developed and are increasing, I think wisely. You use them at your own risk. In theory the Code may be right but in practice flashing exists and we have to live in the traffic world around us.

1. To confirm to someone waiting in a side road to your left that you are pulling up to allow him to join the main road in front of you. You only flash while you are stopped or almost and in the knowledge no-one can overtake you.

2. Similarly to confirm that you wish a driver from the opposite direction waiting positioned to turn right, to cross in front of you.

3. Where you are waiting to turn right off a main road through nose-to-tail traffic (which will lose nothing by waiting while you turn), you can often induce courtesy by switching on your lights. The usual reply saying, "Yes, in front of me" is a short return flash. Traffic clogged behind you is freed from a senseless build-up as a bonus.

4. In faster traffic, when in the same waiting position, keeping headlamps on may alert the fastard who overtakes towards you, apparently unaware you are stopped!

5. When towing, driving a long or wide cargo, etc., use daytime headlights. Police, fire engines and ambulances often use daytime headlights.

6. Constant on-off flashing is used to warn oncomers that there has been an accident behind you, or, at night, that there is some unlit obstruction, e.g. children on horseback without lights.

7. Some people flash to warn you of a radar police trap but this is illegal.

8. Lorry drivers appreciate a flash from you when they overtake to signal to them directly it is safe for them to move in. Without help they may have to judge by "feel"; if it's a slow pass remember you may not be in a position to see some new danger forcing them in.

Unfortunately, flashes as in 1 and 2 above are occasionally used by ignorant drivers, or drivers adhering to the "letter" of the Highway Code to mean the opposite, i.e. "You stop—I'm coming through". You must, therefore, never trust such signals unless confirmed by the driver concerned slowing down: you must also be sure no-one is passing him.

Before flashing the giver has the duty to think on behalf of everyone who will see the flash to ensure none might mis-interpret it.

Beware of your "come-on" flash to a distant motorist which could invite into danger someone nearer and unexpected by you or unexpected by someone else.

TRAFFIC LIGHT KNOWLEDGE
When loaded transport vehicles head the queue at lights they are slow away and rarely mind smaller fry using narrow spaces to squeeze to the front ready to go at green. It is safer if there is room before the line for you to cautiously edge your bonnet slightly ahead so that the heavy vehicle driver sees you (especially on his near-side) before green comes up. It also enables you to see last minute pedestrians. Wherever queues of traffic wait tightly side by side this advanced technique can be applied, for example pelican crossings and other hold-ups, however you must be *certain* the road is clear before getting out ahead at green.

In explaining the above concept I am not suggesting that you risk breaking the law or driving contrary to the advice of the Highway Code. At an uncontrolled zebra crossing with zig-zag lines for example you must not, within the zig-zag area, overtake the moving vehicle nearest the crossing or the leading vehicle which has stopped for someone to cross. The Highway Code warns you not to overtake on the approach to *any* type of pedestrian crossing and this would include pelican crossings as well as ordinary traffic lights many of which allow a special phase for walkers. The idea is not therefore a licence to overtake which could lose you your licence! You will have to judge for yourself whether moving up alongside or perhaps edging a fraction ahead of a waiting vehicle could be construed in any way as overtaking.

The Green Pelican

With the increased number of pelicans found on dual carriageways the matter of overtaking on their approach side can be a trap for the unwary. If both lanes of traffic are full and flowing along towards the crossing drivers will naturally be looking out for pedestrians and a potential change to red. If no-one is waiting and green is likely to persist should you, in the outside lane, if you are in any case overhauling vehicles in the inside lane, carry on with what amounts to an overtake as you approach the immediate vicinity of the crossing? No! The law-abiding advanced driver times himself to maintain maximum vision and to be a little back from and certainly no more than alongside at the lights. His judgement bears in mind that people behind him will probably have no idea of why he is adjusting speed.

In much the same way at ordinary traffic lights lanes of traffic go through together. Despite the Highway Code the world rolls on! The advanced driver again watches that he is not actually overtaking and indeed regards the traffic to one side of him partly as a shield from traffic which might jump the lights across him. He is ready to move ahead instantly he is through the junction and indeed has probably held his relative position to the traffic flowing alongside in such a way as to maximise his vision looking out for stray pedestrians and whatever to his right and left and on the far side of the junction.

Using Green Efficiently

If all drivers used green smartly to help more people get through, the saving in congestion would be enormous—but every little helps! The box junction principle is excellent at lights. Equally essential is "snap" when "go" comes. Dreaming and dawdling at green by a driver can rob six of their chance to go through safely. Multiply that when two or three snails happen to be together! Another way to increase the numbers going through on green is for traffic to close up any unduly long gaps.

Going Fast Through Green On Wide Empty "Through" Routes

Going through fast on green can be dangerous but with

local knowledge of phasing, confirmed by a change to green, a brisk speed may be safe. Very advanced driving needs brains. Not only must your eyes flash to cover both crossing roads, etc., long before reaching them, but your approach positioning is vital.

It should be no risk to take green at 40 m.p.h. if you know it will be green when you reach the area and there is nothing waiting to cross. Where there are cars waiting to the right or left of the yellow box area the risk potential is entirely different. If traffic waiting is only on the left and the junction is otherwise clear a brisk speed may still be reasonable though not as fast as if there were no crossing traffic waiting. The secret is to keep well away from the traffic waiting on the left. You should never chop the numbers off their number plates! Suppose one of them had a foot slip off the clutch or brake—which happens— you would be in trouble! With waiting vehicles on both sides but otherwise safe and you know the lights will stay green the game is to go through the middle well clear of trouble, however remote, with speed adjusted downwards to allow for the increased risk. You thus maximise what we can call your "swerve to safety" area. But the iron rule stands: *Never drive at a speed at which you cannot stop safely in the area you see clear ahead of you.*

Keep a finger at the horn, a foot hovering over the brake and (need I say!) the eyeballs swivelling. Alert, disciplined, fast driving can be safe. It is sleep-drivers who kill people.

The majority of green lights have to be taken at reduced speed because of traffic. Be ever alert for the maniac who comes at 80 m.p.h. when he ought to be at 28, or shoots the red in front of you.

If for some reason you can't stop in time for red (for example brake failure) and have to go through, or slide half across, hoot and flash lights to warn everybody, as the ambulance driver would.

ONE-WAYS

Traffic in one-way systems—tunnels—roundabouts—etc., tends to stagnate where it meets another traffic flow.

One secret here is, where safe, to pre-select the lane likely to have the least traffic or the fewest places where you have to "give way" to people from the right. Prior knowledge of your road can be tapped with advantage on reaching congested areas. Sometimes postponing changing lane until you have passed round bunched traffic helps. By-pass traffic-clots with the brain, not the ill-mannered toe!

FIRST EXAMPLE OF THE ADVANTAGES OF USING THE LANE LEAST LIKELY TO BE HELD UP

One-Way Underpasses

In underpasses—keep right. Most underpasses have two lanes. At the end where other traffic joins it usually has to come in from the left. The road may then temporarily have three lanes to accommodate the extra traffic or alternatively precedence for the underpass traffic may be established by a dotted give-way line. Either way drivers in the left lane of the underpass need to exercise greater care, firstly because the side wall masks the view till the last moment and secondly allowance has to be made for fools swinging directly out into their lane without looking. Even when there is a give-way line drivers will take risks and ease over it regardless.

All this potential or actual drama slows traffic in the left underpass lane. Drivers may even have to stop if cars are trying to push in from the left and the right lane is full of traffic, preventing moving to it. Right lanesters flow smoothly by contrast having less direct contact with merging traffic.

Suppose you are reaching the end of a busy city underpass travelling in the right hand lane but knowing that you will want to turn left fairly soon. If a car is travelling beside you on your left continue in the right lane but keep an eye on it because it will be almost sure to have to slow up in the stagnation explained above. If he doesn't there is a good chance one following him will have to. This leaves the left lane empty long enough for you to ease over for your left turn. Equally, merging in traffic tends to begin cautiously and this usually allows the opportunity to cross to the left as you pass them.

All rules sometimes trap the unwary. In the same instance as above, if the left turn you want came too soon the advantages could be lost. You might get stuck trying to cross over without squeezing anyone and have to take the honourable alternative. That is go on till a suitable opportunity occurred to turn left later. Imagine the turn you wanted was at a traffic light and the queue for the

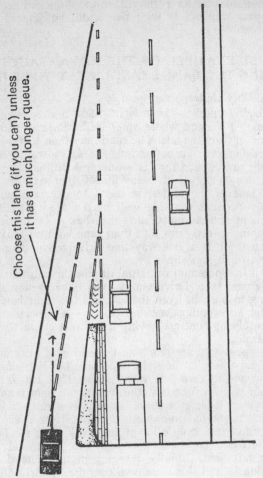

Choose this lane (if you can) unless it has a much longer queue.

Fig. 18. By-passing a stagnation point.

lights started back towards or in the underpass; it would probably be wiser to choose the left lane in the tunnel.

The game is to avoid direct "conflict" with traffic merging in on you where possible.

The principle can be applied in part when you are on the joining in road if it has two lanes as in Fig. 18. Unless it has a much longer queue the left hand lane is the better one to choose. From the left you have a much greater angle of vision and thus more time to see if you can merge in without having to stop. Traffic in the right hand lane usually meets emerging underpass traffic at a sharper angle and, as it also has a harder task to see, is almost bound to have to stop or come nearer to a stop than you on the left will need. Sometimes, while those on your right are stopping or have done, underpass traffic wavers with uncertainty leaving a gap for you to slip into—once again by-passing the stagnation point.

SECOND EXAMPLE OF USING THE LANE LEAST LIKELY TO BE HELD UP

Multi-Lane City Roundabouts

Fig. 19 is typical of a spacious, but traffic blocked, city roundabout. At the entry the right lane is stuck as it has to give way to the packed traffic on its way round. Meanwhile there is empty space round the outer lane of almost the whole of the rest of the roundabout. The space is there for anyone who uses the left entry lane. Room exists to get round safely, following the dotted path in Fig. 19 provided that you keep an eye open, ready to give way, should one of the stagnant drivers decide to leave the roundabout before you do.

If you wish to transfer to the lane next to the edge of the roundabout island there is no obligation to do so at an early stage. Without being too clever you can "play it along". Variation of speed is the key, *looking out that traffic immediately in front does not stop!* Sometimes a touch of acceleration in the appropriate gear allows safe switching ahead of another car. Other times decelerating with maybe a touch of the brake enables you to slip courteously behind someone.

After entering by the left lane to avoid the stagnation of the right hand one, sometimes your only reason for changing from the outside to the inside lane going round is to avoid stagnation at a future entry where more traffic may be pushing in.

The advanced driver uses opportunities with skill but without risk or discourtesy. *If a ploy fails he accepts the punishment of going round once again.*

By using his brains the advanced driver avoids being an unnecessary part of congestion, holds up no-one and filters

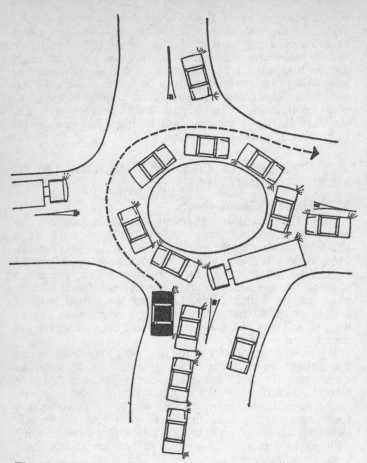

Fig. 19. Making use of empty space at a roundabout.

ahead to release more space (which he would have occupied) for other people behind.

I can visualise some road safety buffs leaping out of their cars in rage but one aim of very advanced driving is the release of every possible road space to promote the progress of all.

If you are no longer there you are not holding anyone up! Some may be jealous of the advantage you have gained but education should teach that jealousy is childish.

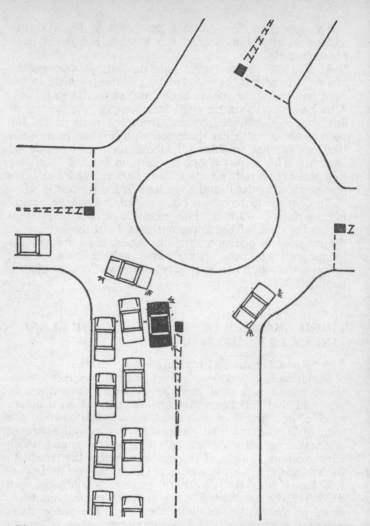

Fig. 20. Another roundabout technique.

There is no need to be unfair. You must not take advantage of others who have positioned by the "accepted" rules. All you are doing is keeping out of their motoring lives by better driving.

An opposite effect to that described in Fig. 19 may happen at city roundabouts and a slightly different technique is useful.

As Fig. 20 shows traffic halts instead, in two queues mainly on the left, aggravated by the front vehicle in the right hand of these queues having pulled too far to his left. This leaves room on his right for an expert. As the last of any group of vehicles coming from the right passes the nose of the expert's car there will be a brief moment while the rear of that vehicle still blocks the badly positioned amateur. This is just about to occur in Fig. 20. It is now that the expert deftly slots his car forward and away. He gets straight to the island edge lane in the process.

Though the technique is often useful, snags have a habit of interfering with it. For example if someone steps across the neck of the approach road from the left just at the moment in question then the expert has a fractionally longer wait while the walker passes and he loses ground; however he does not lose very much and it is usually a good gamble.

THIRD EXAMPLE OF USING THE LANE LEAST LIKELY TO BE HELD UP

The "Road Narrows" Problem

Sometimes a one-way street narrows unexpectedly. Sometimes it is a dual carriageway which thins down or you find that two lanes in your direction on an ordinary road, or in a tunnel or underpass, are whittled down to one with little warning. The game is to watch, well ahead of when you get there, which side reduces width and which edge remains straight. The need is to select the lane with the straight side well in advance. Otherwise you find yourself faced with the choice of squeezing someone (bad driving!) who has "laned" more skilfully, or stopping while those in the unaffected lane sweep by. The reader who grasps the principle will discover many other occasions where the unaffected lane is a winner.

APPROACHING ONE-WAY STREETS

It is essential, if obvious, to look left first when reaching a one-way which flows T-wise across your road from left to right. A check to the right for pedestrians or kids on bicycles flauntingly breaking the rules, must be added. The old ingrained instruction "look right, left and right again" must be reversed here. Otherwise that naughty habit of beginning to nose out once you see it it clear right can land you in a crash from the left.

I say old ingrained instruction because that was the former Highway Code maxim until the introduction of the Green Cross Code for pedestrians. Since then incredibly, the Highway Code, expanded to the point where few people can absorb the welter of instructions and advice, has managed to omit *any* offering on visual safety for drivers emerging from junctions or arriving at same. Those who learned to drive since that minimal advice was dropped I hope will enjoy my later section on systemising a safety eye approach to junctions.

Where a one-way forms the stem of a T leading off your road there is often a "pass either side" arrows bollard placed at the entrance. Many drivers nevertheless enter the one-way only into its left lane. They seem to see but not believe. Advanced drivers pass by such people, by using the road as instructed.

The same drivers will often be found wrongly positioned for turning right when they reach a T at the other end of the one-way. This does not matter if the road to be entered is one-way but if it is two-way and they pull up on the left, while they wait, they succeed in frustrating any following left turners who are positioned correctly. They also look angry if you pull up on their right properly, ready to go right! Avoid such amateur driving. The right edge of these streets should be treated as if it is the crown of the road by those turning right. Let me expose another way time is lost by this.

Both directions of traffic crossing the T politely stop to allow such a wrongly positioned right turner to exit. Because people only wait briefly (incidentally part two of the problem), before some relentless urge to go seems to take charge, anyone baulked behind the amateur and waiting to get away left usually finds there isn't time to move up and come out before main road traffic is again under way. He should have been able to turn left simultaneously and only occupy the same time space. Instead what will probably now have to happen is another group of main road drivers having to stop to let him out. This is how traffic jams are spread!

TRAFFIC FLOW

Even on our busy roads I believe twice as much traffic could flow smoothly if everyone acted for the benefit of the greatest number. Where others keep failing to grasp their gaps (you recognise after following a while) the advanced driver is justified in acting to keep himself moving on so long as there is some benefit to the general flow. Just occasionally however such techniques as I have examined in the preceding pages can be unreasonable or too aggressive. Always temper enthusiasm with fair play. If others are making use of gaps the advanced driver waits. With the continuing horrendous failure of public transport, private traffic ever grows. It is my great hope that skilful driving will keep it moving. Perhaps it is too much to hope also, that when drivers get involved in a minor rear end shunt, they will learn to clear themselves off the carriageway—before a three mile island of jammed traffic forms behind them while they argue the toss.

EASY-WAY FOR ONE-WAYS

In huge wide one-ways, in the event of a scrape, it is usually hard to prove guilt. The dangerous lane is usually the middle one; with vehicles belting along either side you are busy watching them, and have less time to look out in front. At any kerbside obstruction, or cyclist etc., outside lanesters are also liable to squeeze towards your centre lane. Remember, if you get stuck in a fast flowing centre lane temporarily, my "stop or slow in preference to swerving" advice becomes doubly important.

It is safer to keep to one edge where about half your problems are usually eliminated but you must watch well ahead for any chance you will be squeezed towards the kerb. Except where casual parking or lots of turnings off are affecting it I have found the right hand lane generally is the winner. Buppies (page 13) tend to crowd and struggle on the left. Shopping crowds/jaywalkers add risk but where they occur traffic should have slowed right up anyway. In queueing conditions it can help to keep close enough to the pavement to prevent cyclists being tempted to scrape through that side.

TOWN STREETS

In contrast with the main "through" routes, you find in the town streets, on suburban roads and back streets, roads which are usually only one lane each way. These are sometimes a maze of parked vehicles, blind crossroads, roadworks and the other mass junk of suburbia, not to mention their death rôle in and near residential areas which may be children's (unofficial) playgrounds.

KEEPING YOUR DISTANCE

The ideas in this section combined with those under "Bringing Science To Sight" (page 43) form a cornerstone of safe driving.

Alas, one cannot recommend specified distances for drivers spacing themselves behind vehicles ahead. A safe gap cannot be based merely on speed. It is not a gap related to speed alone which is important. The gap has to be under constant review to relate it to the prevailing circumstances. The safe gap by its nature varies from moment to moment.

Many drivers realise this but fail to act on it or else don't have the discipline essential for safety. Prevailing conditions alter every few yards and dangerous situations ahead increase or reduce in degree.

Leaving a gap of the right distance, plus stopping room, is a continuous process; rapidly increasing the gap at every danger risk, however fleeting, allowing it to shorten only as risks diminish. You may reduce the gap for other reasons, perhaps preparing to overtake, but only when safe.

Extending the gap instantly widens your angle of vision, provides yards extra for stopping, and reduces the need for split-second reactions. Gap increasing examples (which should be instinctive):

    a) Before a bend or corner.
    b) Before the brow of a hill.
    c) If the road narrows.
    d) If there are parked vehicles ahead on one side or the other.
    e) Whenever you are following a group of vehicles rather than only one.
    f) If you come up behind a big van, lorry or bus.
    g) Where traffic ahead is knotting up or likely to stop.
    h) Near crossroads, junctions, traffic lights, pedestrian crossings or similar hazards.

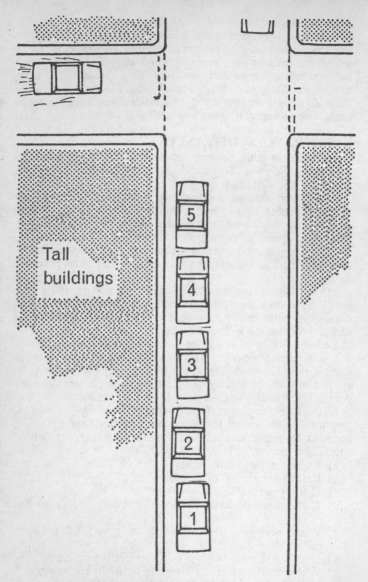

Fig. 21. Four madmen.

i) Wherever pedestrians congregate or there are children or animals loose around.

j) When someone behind, particularly a motorcycle, is threatening to overtake and may need extra room.

The list could go on; *the thing is to become a gap-adjusting driver*!

Do not be intimidated by the back bumper bumper. Your gap in front is *your* life-saver.

A list of safe places for reducing your gap might read:

a) After the road splits into dual carriageway.

b) If the car ahead is easy to see over, round, or through, and obviously well driven.

c) Where buildings are well back from the road or railings fence off any children. The list could continue.

To re-emphasise (and this is rarely stressed) the secret is variation . . . the bigger the risk the longer the gap. And more and more so as speed increases.

Think of the gap you must constantly adjust as the "stopping and thinking gap". Fig. 21 shows four madmen. The fifth is sane but helpless at the front. The crossroads at the top is a frightening blind danger area. The four by keeping nose-to-tail are restricting their own view of any risks and if number five had to jam on (as he well may) a six-vehicle pile up would be almost certain.

Compare this with the wisdom and vision of the wise drivers in Fig. 22 as they approach the same situation.

They understand "thinking time". (The time-lag between the moment the chap in front brakes, or crashes, and your reaction.) Each, by increasing his "stopping and thinking" gap, and/or by positioning to one side of the line taken by the car ahead, is leaving himself room to stop.

Keeping away from danger is the heart of safety, even if the danger is half-a-mile off. At the first sniff of trouble the very advanced driver extends his gap so removing the likelihood of being caught needing panic stations action.

It is for all these situations where several cars may be nose-to-tail behind him that the advanced driver may wish to consider fitting an extra pair of ordinary brake lights (not high intensity red rear lamps) wired to operate with his ordinary brake lamps but rigged high inside the back window. Being high these can be seen by drivers several places behind when your waist level ones would not be. In addition they give twice the warning to any fellow right

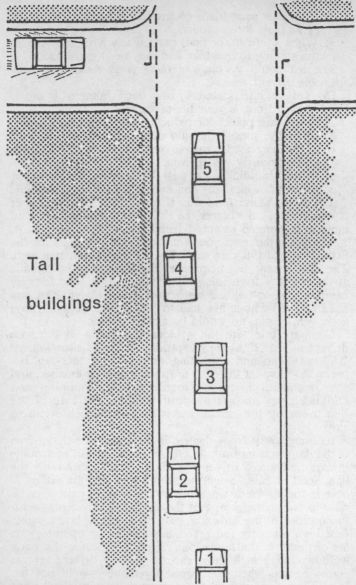

Tall

buildings

Fig. 22. Five sane men.

on your boot. Care must be taken to follow the lighting regulations exactly brake lights can only be added as a pair and they must be of the prescribed type, fitted the regulation distance apart and only up to a certain height above the ground. The latest regulations can always be checked with the Department of Transport. You must bear in mind that a vast battery of brake lights on the back would not be allowed since this could contravene the requirements of driving with due care and attention for other road users.

HOW A SIGNAL CAN BANISH DOUBT

In fig. 23 you may at first think your road is straight on but then the back of the Give Way notice or a tell-tale line shows your right-hand bend. Because of the layout the white car

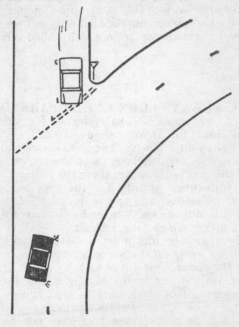

Fig. 23. Positioning, *and* a signal, to alert a driver in doubt. The two main points discussed in the text are, 1) the need for the black car to give a signal, 2) positioning so it is obvious where you are going.

may conclude you will be forking left and come straight on out. The advanced driver selects his line so as to make it obvious he is going round, as well as adding an indicator signal. This removes doubt, alerts and advises. The positioning is advanced; plus the signal--very advanced! You will also be wise to toot, slow up and be considering your swerve/stop options until you see that he has seen you, or failed to, as the case may be!

At any junction if there is continuous traffic from his *left* while someone waits to turn right into a main road you are coming along from his right, it is unlikely he will move. But watch out if he sees there will soon be a gap . . . lest he shoots forward before checking your direction.

The thing to look for whenever someone is waiting (or arriving) to emerge from a side turning is not merely whether he looks your way. It's how long, and how thoroughly, that matters. Watch his face for "recognition" if you can. Never trust the hurried glance, nor the obviously stiff-necked driver. You must be certain you are not in his blind spot (see page 81).

DO YOU ALWAYS LOOK UNDER PARKED CARS?

We learn to watch below vehicles for feet, prams, etc., and check for anyone about to open the door, but few manage to do it always. The good driver grabs chances to check as they arise. Seizing these fleeting views is a hall-mark of the master. However there has to be an alternative because sometimes priority for the eyes to concentrate elsewhere coincides and prevents such chances being grasped. It is slow down! Your sub-conscious should shout it to you; give yourself time, instead.

Fig. 24 dramatises the point. In 24 (a) you see tell-tale feet from 50 yards off, before you reach a parked car. At 25 yards they have gone out of view, as in (b). The scenario from the other direction (c), highlights the, far from un-usual, unseen horror battle for a football, with at least one child liable to be tipped into your path at any second.

There will be times when you have not had time to check underneath and you reach a position such as (b). You must then take into account whether anyone is coming towards you for you will have virtually nil stopping power if a child pops out; most of your hope would lie in being

78

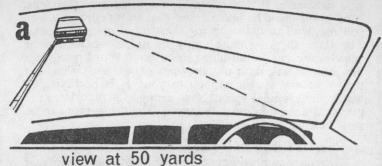

view at 50 yards

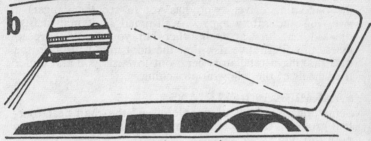

nothing looks amiss
at 25 yards

view from the other direction

Fig. 24. Looking under parked cars.

able to swerve. If there is traffic the other way therefore, your speed must be much more drastically curbed before you reach (c) to make up for the lack of swerving room. The same thinking must apply in streets where cars or vehicles are parked all along. You can't afford to assume that no-one will dash out between parked cars. One day they will; and it will happen to you! It is horrifying to watch the criminal speeds that a minority of drivers are prepared to risk in our city streets. The death race can be won well under 30 m.p.h.

Hooting On Behalf Of Others

When coming the other way in a Fig. 24 type of situation you may save life by keeping in to your own side to leave the oncoming driver (who has yet to see the danger) a swerving and safety gap. A well-timed hoot may defuse the kiddies' fury at each other but you would have to assess the alternative risk that the hoot might result in the kids making a retaliatory leap out towards you and under the wheels of the fellow approaching.

SWARMING PEDESTRIANS

Sometimes hundreds of people crowd the road near football grounds, race meetings, in market streets; etc. To help nose through:
a) Switch on headlights.
b) Politely request "thank you" out of the window.
c) Hold the clutch down and with gear in neutral, rev the engine . . . brroom! brrrroom! brrrrooom! Don't hoot. That's not "cricket". Humour is your best bet. After all, you can't mow them down! Rightly or not they feel they have as much right on the street as you.

HIDDEN MONSTERS

Imagine you are going up a wide main road which shortly passes through a crossroads. Someone coming the other way suddenly whirls right, slap across your bows to get down the side road which is to your left. Watch for the double danger! While you brake to miss the first idiot another, in the shape of a motorbike or a small car previously hidden from you behind the front vehicle, commits himself to swing across you as well, leaving almost no chance to avoid a smash. You are not blameless; you should have braked *more* than just enough to miss the first idiot till you saw whether the second was there.

BLIND SPOTS

The natural blind spot of the eye in relation to driving has received little publicity. Fig. 25 demonstrates it. Add to this limitation of the eye itself the blind spots due to door pillars, mirrors, driving licence holders, dirt or greasy smears on the screen, etc., and you can see why at junctions and roundabouts one quick look and away is not enough. In certain directions despite the fact you look you do not always see. It is the second (or even the third) sweeping look that picks out the things blind spots hide.

It is imperative that you look long enough to focus, and concentrate sufficiently to see movement. Otherwise a second look will also fail to pick up anything previously hidden. Do not be ashamed, or too lazy, to swivel the head, neck and shoulders forward, back, any way necessary to avoid (for lack of a better word) being "blind-spotted".

In heavy rain, drops on the side windows mask vision, so open sufficiently to see. Open more at night, when seeing is harder.

At junctions, physically moving your head to look round the door pillars on either side is *essential*. It is lack of blind spot understanding that has led to the massive increase in accidents with bicycles and motor cycles.

Fig. 25. Natural eye blind spots
Look at the steering wheel on the **right,** and close your right eye. Hold the book about a foot away from your **left** eye, straight in front of it. At approximately this distance it is impossible to see the wheel on the left while your eye focuses on the one on the right. The distance may be slightly more, or less depending on your eyes. This shows there is a considerable angle of view which the eye cannot cover a built in eye blind spot.

81

Fig. 26 illustrates how even slim door pillars obscure a wide area, being so close to the eye.

SYSTEMISING A SAFETY EYE APPROACH TO JUNCTIONS

We will assume you are not on the main road and will not differentiate between approaching a give way line, a stop line or no line. We are concerned with safety vision. We will take it that you have used your mirror.

Your street is narrow. Buildings, billboards, hedges, etc., at the corners where you meet the crossing road, make the opening blind. With an open-to-view crossroad oppor-

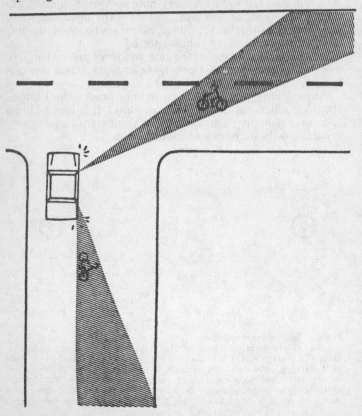

Fig. 26. Door pillar blind spot.

tunities to look one or both ways while approaching would have been taken as they arose. Here—the blind corner— may be a black spot. .

The Deadly Blind Junction

In the last few yards speed is dropped to walking pace, no more—in the last 5 feet to that of a snail. Immediate dangers are likely in the final 10–15 feet before the stopping position. The dance of death usually comes from the left—prams, children racing, youths, dogs, etc. In a flash one may be under you, crushed.

Your devastating braking reaction must beat them to it. The blinder the slower is the motto. You may literally, where the road is very narrow, need to stop, allow a second or two for people to note the bonnet and hope they may hear the engine, and then only, edge forward gently till you see more.

The danger may be less from the right but if anyone is walking across safety and courtesy demand that he has priority. Another right side danger may come from what I term the "kerbside-slinker". Be they on moped or in car these are the sort who tootle along picking up nails in the gutter and give you a fright as they pass inches from your stopping line.

Danger can also hurtle from the left in the form of the driver who cuts across you as he whirls right without having signalled. This is what happens and you must avoid the naughty habit: because you see him bombing along from the left without any signal you begin to assume that he is going straight on and so you move out by a fraction; with every other direction clear and expecting him to pass on the other side at any second you find (if you look at yourself) that you have moved well into your half of the main road simultaneously with your final look to the right. At that point there is a horrendous bang as he swings right oblivious of the fact that he had no signal. I leave you to ponder over who is more to blame.

Systemising approach to dangerous crossroads is therefore not merely "looking right, left and right again" and in the mirror. The requirement is for an all-embracing method integrating this very slow roll stop with efficient anti-blind spot treatment. Every conceivable danger point must be seen by moving head and eyes, taking priorities in order, especially during the last 12 feet.

An example of failure to do it occurred in the "blind" drive entrance to our home; a previous owner told me two cars "met" and five people were taken to hospital.

THE DANGER OF STALLING

A feeling of well being takes hold of many a driver as he sails along the main road. Despite a vehicle emerging from a side road ahead, he continues at his set speed, oblivious to the chance that that driver might stall. If only he would lift his foot off and be prepared for braking, many accidents would be avoided.

The advanced driver can only protect himself from such drivers by making sure that he never stalls. He gets his accelerator going before, as, and after he lets the clutch up, so as to make sure he gets over the danger area safely, quickly. He uses resolute but not ferocious acceleration, always.

If he has used the handbrake he keeps a hand on it so that it cannot be forgotten. He applies the same principle if he is using a manual choke holding it ready to pull or push as required. He is quick to note if the gear lever or the car shudders and stops at once. (Only if there was no other choice would he choose to struggle forward having recognised he was in a mistakenly selected gear.)

Never linger in danger areas or begin to cross them until sure you will succeed and cannot be robbed of space to occupy beyond, out of danger.

If people behind are tooting, it only annoys you if you let it. But be fair because few hoot without reason. They may think you are dreaming instead of concentrating.

Wait for a gap with time to cross at walking speed. You go faster but need that safety margin. The killer is stalling in the face of the main road traffic. Keep your eyes switching left, right and ahead and to wherever danger may lurk, *while crossing*.

When driving along a main road and you see someone ahead pulling across apparently in plenty of time think (not like the half-witted idiot, or the "my speed" types mentioned in chapter 1) "is he going to stall?" Working on the assumption he will, *until it is clear he has not*, will force you to ease speed early. This is the key that enables you to stop in time should the worst happen, and sometimes, it does.

In the event of an accident at least some of the blame is

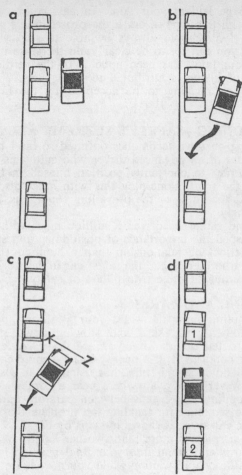

Fig. 27. Parking between cars.

a) Stop beyond the car next the space about 3 ft. outside parallel to it and with the back of your car slightly ahead as shown.
b) Reverse in, very slowly does it, left lock to begin with but not too deeply. Be alive to the danger to other traffic (those ahead especially, *will not* always wait) as your outer corner bonnet starts to swing out.
c) Begin to change steering lock from the line X—Z and aim to be on full lock just as soon as possible after your left front wing clears the parked car.
d) Once "in", adjust to leave equal room in front and behind so that cars 1, and 2, can get out easily.

85

likely to be laid at your door. In past court cases concerned with this type of crash the prosecution's view that, because "you should always be able to stop within the distance you can see to be clear" and therefore it must be partly your fault, has been upheld. In the verdict a percentage of blame is attributed to each party, 20% of it, for example, having to be accepted by the main road driver.

POSITIONING—SAFETY'S SUPREME ALLY

Reflecting on town techniques outlined so far I hope that the picture of an advanced driver who cultivates anticipation in order to constantly position himself in the safest part of the road, combining this with strict discipline of his speed according to the prevailing conditions, is emerging strongly.

I would rather be driven a million miles with a driver who grasped the importance of positioning and speed and their interlocking relationship than a hundred yards with a driver who merely had the safest car in the world but no understanding of these twin pillars of safety.

STOPPING AND PARKING

When pulling into the side, your position line, gently easing towards the kerb and slowing down should be enough to tell others what you are doing. A left flasher however, confirms it. If a nearby turning could confuse, an arm slow-down signal helps, but usually it is wiser not to stop, however briefly, anywhere near a corner.

In shopping areas, gaps between cars are harder to fit into. The sequence for tackling the problem the right way for a one car space is shown in steps by Fig. 27.

When a space is more than two car lengths you can go in forwards and shunt into your final position later. This saves traffic behind waiting while you manœuvre and is an example of very advanced consideration.

Sometimes when you have stopped a little forward of a one car space and are trying to reverse in drivers pull up too close. You are prevented before you've started! To avoid this, stop initially alongside the gap. Don't move forward until the chap behind has stopped. Then, when you nip forward smartly to position (a) in Fig. 27, he should be able to see what you are doing and wait courteously.

Occasionally some cheeky follower seizes the opportunity to drive forward into your space. If this is done intentionally, it is better to treat it with contempt. It is not worth delaying traffic to have a row.

PEDESTRIANS ARE CRACKERS

A pedestrian can be defined as "one who does not know a car can reverse". Despite the warning to pedestrians in the Highway Code that they should not stand behind any vehicle which has its engine running the reality is that when you are reversing shoppers frequently stupidly walk through the decreasing gap between you and the car you are backing up to. Whether they consciously imagine that cars only go forwards or simply assume you are bound to have seen them the fact is that they *do* walk through. Since they won't you *must* take the responsibility for their safety.

MOTTO FOR REVERSING—DON'T

Don't unless you must. Reversing is an unpleasant necessity and because of its dangers wise drivers reverse as little as possible. When forced to reverse, move backwards only enough to make the next forward move, never more. Not one inch more. However, do not be afraid to reverse into an opening if it means it will be safer not to have to reverse out when you leave, for example in a car park or driveway.

Some so-called advanced drivers rely solely on the mirrors when reversing. This is crazy, as any small child will tell you.

TOWN BOTTLENECKS

In the next chapter I discuss village bottlenecks in which traffic in opposite directions finds itself stuck looking at each other. Such moments are made for the advanced thinker, not for the advanced sitter! In narrow town streets it is often the case that the clogging factor in one direction is someone waiting to turn right who cannot do so because the traffic in the other direction has closed up and is sitting straddling the opening into which he wants to turn. Just because they may have been overjoyed to squeeze forward an extra five yards for themselves in their own jam is no excuse for then becoming the prime cause of a two hundred yard jam for people going the other way. The motto in such crawling queues is to think before blocking up an opening that traffic *yet to arrive* in the other direction might want to use.

THE MOVING OBSTRUCTION

There can hardly be a driver who is not aware that the law says you may not park so as to cause an unnecessary obstruction. How many drivers, however, know that they can be prosecuted for obstructing a middle or outside lane where traffic in each direction has more than one lane available to it? Those drivers who imagine that if they are keeping up to the speed limit they are somehow "entitled" to remain in the outside lane, or to sit in the middle lane of three, are dangerously wrong. The rule of the road is to keep to the left except during overtaking or turning right and to allow others to overtake you if they want to. There are special rules about traffic moving in queues and one-ways but the fundamental requirement of allowing others to overtake if they wish is over-riding.

To deliberately obstruct a driver who has indicated his desire to pass by a hoot or a headlight flash, or even merely by coming up behind quickly, is to commit a moving obstruction unless you yourself are in the normal process of overtaking something else or positioning (and signalling!) coming up for a right turn. It is an offence.

Not only does the baulking driver cause intense frustration and temper behind him (and who knows how many apparently quite separate accidents have this as a contributory factor?) he encourages those behind to break the rules by overtaking him on his inside. Such "underpassing" is now so widespread the advanced driver must now be sure before he hoots or flashes to request a car to move over that there is not going to be one of these "underpassers" trying to zip through who will cause an accident as the road-hog moves over.

Apart from more consistent police prosecution of such drivers, particularly on motorways (both the underpassers and the baulkers), I see no easy answer to this growing flashpoint in driving. As a second or subsequent driver waiting to pass you can only await your turn once he finally moves over. If nothing seems to be going to shift a baulking driver after "miles" say, on a motorway, it is usually best to pull back, and over, and wait a while. It saves you ulcers and usually gives a chance to study some bad driving! If you are number two or three or in a group of potential passers a headlight flash from you may be necessary where the front man being baulked is being too timid about letting the obstructing driver know that there is a queue behind; however that's about all you can do.

4

COUNTRY TECHNIQUES

REALLY NARROW LANES

Picture a typical narrow country lane, barely wider than the car, often sunken and with a high grass bank or hedge. Here you are prey to the weekend reveller as much as to the over-confident local who "knows" every blade of grass!

Fig. 28 illustrates a blind hairpin bend with almost no passing room. Unless drivers drop to crawling speed as they reach the bend there is a very good chance that a smash will occur every time two drivers happen to arrive at it together. Assuming that as an advanced driver you will have slowed to a sensible snail's pace, what can you do about people coming the other way?

You can make good use of your horn when within earshot, tuck into your own side and, as well as getting speed down to barely moving, have your brake pedal covered during the tightest, blindest part(s) of the corner. Then keep your focus constantly on the unfolding scene and hope that no young blood without the discipline that wisdom dictates is going to rocket round it. The reason for keeping right in, even if it only leaves a few feet to your outside, is to give any downhill cyclist, such as in Fig. 28, with his head down, room to scrape by and survive.

The anti-horn brigade may demur. Let them. The advanced motorist, without being a public nuisance, keeps in mind the question on accident insurance claim forms: "Did you sound your horn?" which shows the importance those with daily experience of accidents attach to this safety measure. However he or she never relies on the horn. It will not clear the road, as any herd of cows will tell you!

Fig. 28. A blind hairpin bend.

ROADS JUST WIDE ENOUGH FOR TWO CARS

Seemingly innocent curves can conceal death traps, like the boy racer motorcyclist who has leant over to cut the corner, coming the other way. You reach a blind bend and in a trice he is there, more than half-way over on to your side. Although you may not be at fault, if you collide one or both of you may be killed.

Unfortunately the first time you see a skidiot hurtle out of a corner towards you can be the one that lands you in hospital. It is no use either, driving on winding roads cosily assuming that the only problem you might meet will be another car. You must keep imaginative and be ready to find the Devil seeking his opportunity in a steam-roller, a late delivery van, or even a junior devil on a soap-box cart!

No driver can be proof against every such thing but the advanced driver is rigidly disciplined about how he slows down for this sort of corner in order to be in instant command should evasive action be necessary. He won't allow himself to be "pushed" too fast into a bend. On faster corners he may also be observed slowing down more than a fool behind might like but once on to the next straight he does not mind accelerating to the fellow's heart's content. More than likely however, if it's a decent straight with nothing coming, he will slow up and let him pop by.

Suppose through racing down a narrow road you killed a child who was coming out of a hidden bridle path as quickly as you might have swatted a fly, think how the sadness would lay upon your conscience. Thinking about potential consequences requires a conscious effort no worthy advanced motorist can dismiss. To let someone

90

behind menace you into undue speed is not on, any more than would be your own recklessness.

Returning to the narrowest of lanes it is best on right hand bends, while watching for the odd rock sticking out, to keep close to the left edge. It is sometimes helpful as the corner unfolds to lean over to your left to see better. As you approach a blind left bend there is some advantage in keeping a little out from the edge, when your speed is reasonable. Oncomers see you earlier, as you do them, and you see pedestrians, dogs, etc., on your own side sooner. However if doing this the obligation is upon you to be slow enough to be able to brake and pull in to your side, allowing for weather and conditions, should someone approach. You would have no right to rob his road.

In country lanes you sometimes meet streams of approaching traffic. As well as watching that *you* may not have to move out slightly to avoid a boulder or tree root, you should scan their side. The driver who is more intent on caring for his car than his life will swing over for the smallest pothole! Depending on space available you may need to be ready to slow up or stop. In narrow conditions grip the wheel tightly; then if you misjudge and hit a rock you will be less likely to bounce off into worse danger. In tight circumstances keeping your car parallel with the approaching vehicles helps you to ease past.

Sometimes on a narrow road such as we have been discussing you are suddenly faced—over a brow for example—with a car coming into view and a motorcycle hard on its exhaust pipe, perhaps even nudging its way past the car. Even where it may not "theoretically" be up to you to give way, quick action is sometimes the only way to save an accident. Were the other car to brake the bike would be almost certain to run into the back of him and the rider be thrown off; or, if the bike rider tried to brake fast, he could equally finish up thrown under your wheels. Whereas if you brake and "positionally" show what you are doing by nosing tight into your side: (a) it allows seconds extra thinking and dropping back time for the motorcycle and (b) it removes doubt from a dangerous situation both for him and the other car (who at once knows that he may not need to brake).

The advanced rule to follow for all similar situations is that if it is easier and safer for you to do the braking than than for the others, *do it*.

Crossroads In Country Lanes

Crossroads are sometimes not marked for priority so you have to assume neither road has it. Stop until sure it is safe. To maximise vision lie out a little when blind to the left but clear to see right or keep left if the right is more obscured. This is the advanced art of manufacturing extra vision by positioning. A hoot as you start across can save you from the unforeseeable.

MAIN ROADS CROSSING THE COUNTRYSIDE

Now wider roads: the A and B routes varying between ample two-way width, occasional three lanes (two-way) and dual carriageways.

LEAVING ROOM FOR OTHERS TO OVERTAKE

Suppose you are part of a traffic stream with no wish to overtake. As stream speed increases an advanced driver also goes faster but he quickly allows the gap ahead of him to expand allowing space for faster traffic to pass into. Should such a gap be temporarily filled by the first car to pass he allows another one to develop. Otherwise a bunch of selfish nose-to-tail drivers forms and faster cars can only pass at risk to themselves as well as others. Behind a lorry they may have to wind on for miles. Consideration for others is the essence of good driving manners. The advanced driver happily helps faster drivers leap-frog him one by one, by faster thinking.

Even if an overtaking car does not use a gap it must be left at his disposal. Otherwise the driver who did not leave it could be part III of an accident.

Part II of such an accident would probably be an oncoming motorist who stuck to his "rights" and gave no leeway to the overtaking driver. The original fault would be with the overtaking driver for failing to make sure he had a clear passage to pass *and a gap to go into* but apportioning blame to the dead is a useless task!

Perhaps the most culpable because he could have done something about it would be the fool who insisted on his "rights". At the first sight of such a situation he ought to have instantly signalled left, pulled into his side and braked, to a stop if need be.

Instantaneous braking in potential danger keeps the car balanced and under control ready for that second later when real danger may exist. One is ready for necessary evasive action—perhaps even driving off the road to the left. If there was a high kerb this would necessitate a tight grip on the wheel and mounting the kerb at an angle to prevent being kicked back. Do anything to avoid the head-on killer.

The immediate left indicator signal: (a) tells the oncoming nutcase you have seen him and (b) you will be pulling in to the left. You thus decide for him which way he must turn and with luck you will probably instil in him the confidence he will need to pass through the danger of his own creation.

THE NIGHTMARE THREE LANES, TWO-WAY
Including many wide roads which, although marked as one lane each way, are used like the three lane roads.

Bends To The Right
On a right hand bend where the distance you can see is limited stay well over in the left of the three lanes. This keeps you away from trouble if heavy traffic is coming the other way. It gives earlier vision of any fool coming who is bent on passing on the corner and who is otherwise masked by the leading traffic—particularly the hairy motorcyclist! Where another driver in front of you goes round with his car in the middle of the road (or a madman overtakes you) keep well left and a long way behind him, to allow yourself a space to keep out of any accident.

On the other hand at a right hand bend, sometimes visibility shows all is clear for half a mile and this gives the good driver a really safe chance to pass.

Bends To The Left
Keep well left but not so close that if you have to pass a cyclist you need to swing out. Keeping too close in may tempt someone to overtake at a dangerous time. If someone does try be ready to brake or accelerate as required in order to let him cut back to save his life and maybe yours!

Disappearing Gap
Sometimes when you are being overtaken the gap which the passer intends to use melts away because traffic ahead begins to slow up for some reason. If you are the one committed to overtake it is a pretty frightening thing to happen.

You may have to brake heavily to keep a gap for some-one caught like this. If you judge that he has realised that he must fall in behind you on the other hand, you may have to temporarily speed up before slowing because of the traffic ahead. Keep your wits. If someone attempts to cut in front of you, for whatever reason, do not accelerate—let him in. Only madmen accelerate risking head on, death accidents which can kill innocent and guilty.

"Steering" Message.

An approaching middle lanester (or someone yet afar off but showing signs of nosing out) may be helped if you can move in slightly to confirm you will be happy. Drivers behind you also see what's afoot sooner. But think twice before trying to help; an over-hasty driver behind could see your move simultaneously as one inviting *him* to swing out . . .

Double White Lines

Crossing a line you should not is breaking the law unless to avoid an accident or pass round a stationary obstruction. An element of feeling safer affects some drivers when they are happily inside double lines. Their concentration wanes. They react slowly and follow blindly. In case one snores behind you when you have to pass a cyclist or small obstruction while keeping within the lines, use your indicator even though it may seem unnecessary. It should wake him up! It is doubly important at night and wherever the road is narrow—even if there are no double lines.

Fig. 29 shows an arrangement of double lines which often replaces the free-for-all of two-way traffic on a three-lane carriageway. It is easy to be lulled into thinking

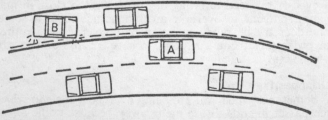

Fig. 29. Illusory double white lines.
Driver A, LOOK OUT! for driver B.

no-one will come out of the single lane in the opposite direction when you are in the outer passing lane of the two-lane side.

What you must watch for is any stretch where that single lane has a dotted line on its own side entitling drivers to come out if safe. Alas, some come out when it is *not* safe, so to keep alive, keep alert.

HERRING BONE LINES

Diagonal lines are sometimes marked on a main road as in Fig. 30 where there is a turn off. They form an elongated "island". Most drivers assume the hatched part creates a "no-go" area. In part they are wrong. The lines around the edge of the hatched shape have gaps in, so one *can* go on the striped area. It is better not to for the most part because the entire "island" is intended as a safe refuge for those turning right—protection from being hit in the back or by anyone coming. However the exception is when you are moving into the "shielded" right turn position; for this purpose the earlier you get over the easier it is for followers to filter past on your left and for anyone further behind to see your signal in good time. To achieve these benefits there is no harm in running on the striped area. Some would say it's madness not to!

While shelter is provided by these areas for the deadly right turn off fast roads you still need to watch for the overtaking nut coming up in front or behind; be ready to use horn, headlights, flash brake lights or in the last resort drive out of the way. Whenever you turn right off a high-speed road, whether with the comfort of herring bone

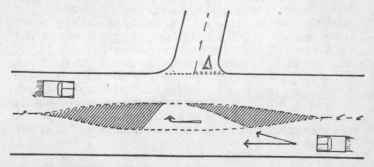

Fig. 30. Herring bone lines.

95

shelter lines or not, keep your front wheels straight ahead during any waiting in the middle before completing the turn. Then if you are shunted, at least it may not be into oncoming traffic.

WHERE YOUR SIDE ROAD CROSSES A MAIN ROAD

Fact: Whilst in a main road traffic stream few drivers heed crossroad warning signs as they drive through fast. Some are sleep-drivers. You court death if you risk stalling (see page 84) or delay during crossing. Avoid being caught in the middle (see below) and *never drive across anyone's safe stopping distance*. If you are crossing the first half of a dual carriageway hoping to pause in the gap before going on over the second half, be certain before you start that you will not be leaving your boot hanging behind in the fast lane or your bonnet poking out into the next one. You dare not assume you will only have a short wait. One day a sleep-driver will get you.

At an ordinary junction if a car waits opposite to come straight over you can both cross at once. If he is turning right he has to go behind you in theory, as at any crossroad, whether you are going right or across. In practice, many attempt to beat you by nipping across your bows. Situations vary but this is likely when main road traffic from the left clears before that from the right—which holds you at the edge of your road—and the chap opposite grasps the chance to get half-way out for his right turn before you can move.

Showing the fellow over the other side your right turn signal before traffic clears ought to prevent trouble, but he may pay no attention, or there may be an instant gap in the traffic and no time for him to register what you are trying to show. If you are both turning right it may be that the lay-out of the junction suits passing left side to left side and that you must be ready for this. Your right turn signal only tells him you are going to turn right. You can in addition "positionally" advise him that when the chance comes you are ready to pass left side to left side. Fig. 31 shows one danger of this however; you must look out for any motorcyclist about to burst out from behind him, now revealed in my picture.

The secret is to try to establish what he will do before you move. Otherwise you can get tied together in the

Fig. 31. Positional driving.

middle at the mercy of "fastards" and sleep-drivers on the main road, who "won't" realise you may both be in a fix.

Not only that, some non-thinking idiot behind you usually closes up directly you move forward and robs you even of a space to reverse back to—this latter sin being one I hope no reader of this book will ever again commit!

HOW IT MAY BE POSSIBLE TO SAVE TIME WHEN YOU JOIN A MAIN ROAD

Where the entry to a main road is wide and the view both ways is open as you reach the junction it may be safe to move on to the main road without a stop. Often readiness to do this saves minutes. For example by keeping going you may be able to join the road ahead of a slow car safely. Had you stopped first, in the few seconds lost the car would have become too close. Behind the slow car could be a long stream. But look out!—when turning left someone from *that* direction may be in the process of overtaking and coming fast on your side of the road.

The technique at such junctions is to cut speed earlier than usual during your approach to the line. About 20 yards from it your speed should be little more than walking pace. This gives you time for advance glances to confirm if it will be safe to turn without a stop. If clear, a

97

few yards are then still left in which to regather speed.

At a dual carriageway (where his signal cannot be misinterpreted) the awake main road driver can help too. As he comes along—if he knows he is your only obstacle—he can wink right and move to the outside lane. If in it already he can add a couple of right winks to show you he's happy about you pulling out. With a single outside lanester still a long way off you may decide to go on before having such handy confirmation. Put his mind at rest as you do so, by clinging closer to the nearside edge than usual—so that he sees you will not wander into his outside lane path.

THE VILLAGE BOTTLENECK
A few main roads still have to pass through quaint old villages. Ancient hanging signs or picturesque corners of buildings may lean out above a road still as narrow as a century ago. One expects "snarl-ups" to occur but they are made much worse by drivers who sit in the queue with their motoring-minds vacant.

Queues in both directions sometimes seem to get interlocked. Until the blockage is released at one end, no-one can move at the other. For example a lorry may be unable to squeeze through a very narrow part of a street until a car alongside queueing in the other direction has moved on. But that car cannot move on because of a similar bottleneck ahead of him at the other end of the jam.

A few alert drivers can save the day. Suppose a jam happens and you are caught somewhere in the middle. Keep a look-out further up the line, and behind you. Frequently, by moving a few inches on or back, or into the edge or on to the pavement, you can allow the cars nearest you to move as well. It's often a small movement like this which can make it possible for someone stuck along the line to release himself and in turn for the blockage to clear. Once one end of a bottleneck is released the other is usually clear soon. If a long jam is being caused by undue dithering it can be helpful to get out and handwave nervous drivers through a safe space.

TALKING AND LOOKING AT THE COUNTRYSIDE
Some people can talk and simultaneously concentrate on driving. *Others cannot.* You have to be honest with yourself because even the brilliant at it need to quit conversing

during difficult situations. Gazing at the scenery (or birds by the road) is suicidal and a danger to others. Sharpen up your self-discipline if you have grown into naughty habits.

"GUESSWORK" NAVIGATION

Fix in your mind before starting, the relative position of each town you go to as compared with the previous and the next and you shouldn't miss the road even if you miss the sign. Knowing that town "Y" is way down to the left of town "X" on the map enables you to pick the right road out of town "blindfold". Passengers marvel how you always seem to know!

SUMMARY OF POLICY

1) Systemize the way you watch each relevant detail and hazard you approach. If your main road flows across another side road for example, and you cannot see right at first but the left has an open view, check the left. Having taken note of any traffic on the left and adjusted speed and position accordingly this should leave you free to look to the right directly it comes into view.

2) Constantly relate your speed and position to what you can see, moment to moment.

3) With other cars ahead as you all approach a hazard, discipline yourself to maintain enough safety margin around you. Increase your "thinking and stopping" gap perhaps, or keep to one side of the line taken by whoever is immediately ahead, or both. Both disciplines let you see more, and both "manufacture" stopping room.

PLAN THE WAY YOU READ THE ROAD—ADJUST SPEED AND POSITION TO ACCOUNT FOR THE UNFOLDING SCENE—MAINTAIN A "COCOON" OF SAFE AREA ALL ROUND.

If one could literally visualise such a "cocoon" its size would be infinitely variable, increasing obviously with speed, reduced visibility, in fast-moving traffic, etc., but less obviously with factors like poor night vision, tiredness (a major undocumented cause of accidents), depression, family squabbles or other emotional turmoils, the need for a loo stop and so on which should all be brought into the allowances you make.

FIRST SNIFF BRAKING

The faster you drive the more important it is to bring the car under control at the first sniff of a hazard.

Any idiot can speed; the hard thing is to stop when you have to. When you spot that sniff of danger up ahead *cut speed first*. You can always speed up if it is nothing but if it is bad news you are already in braking equilibrium and it may have saved your life. If you are still in trouble, remember a hoot in time may change disaster into breathing space, should there be, for example, any chance of stopped traffic being able to move forward.

Two very advanced moments for first sniff braking spring to mind: 1) with a left-hander ahead, as any oncoming cars come into view watch their side panels. Tell-tale reflections of brake lights can give that once-in-a-million warning of a sudden hold-up round the corner. 2) With sunshine streaming across a sunken lane you often see the shadow first of anyone coming. If you know there is an obstruction such as a cyclist for them to pass round ... that shadow is *your* first sniff!

5

OVERTAKING

REDUCE TIME EXPOSURE TO DANGER

The minimum exposure to danger, on the off, wrong, side of the road, should be the aim on each overtake. Maximise acceleration taking the best gear in advance to avoid the risky problem of having to change gear during the overtake and so that both hands can be on the wheel throughout the pass as they need to be. The correct gear should give ample reserve of speed. To pass without any acceleration in reserve (other than perhaps in a "flying pass"   see page 110) is to court disaster.

PREPARATORY EYE WORK

On a typical "B" road there may only be one chance in several miles, requiring considerable advanced guile to spot it. One tip may be to move in left (cautiously; there might be a cyclist) to see past along the inside of the vehicle in front. Another way to get a better view along the inside is to increase the gap between you first. This same gap principle is what builds in safety to the more obvious task of seeing round the off-side and away up ahead. It is the essential ingredient which saves you having to pull out much, if at all.

Be unafraid of moving position relative to other traffic in the stream at this preparatory stage. Although you must watch the mirror and you must not scare oncoming traffic—there is no need to be hidebound by custom. Place your car on any safe inch of space available that helps provide the best view.

Because this pre-view is a continuing process during which miles of road may be covered if you get few chances, it may only be possible at the first or any one check, for example along the inside, to decide something along these lines: "Okay. Road clear with nothing to cause this man to swing out for at least six hundred yards until the next bend." You thus inform yourself that all other factors being in favour, you might get a chance to pass safely during this "time limit". It means equally that you know you will have to re-check once it expires. Alternatively, your first peep may show that there is no hope of passing and tell you that you must wait until you reach the bend before another check will be appropriate. Sometimes that first look along the inside is used (and is vital) merely to establish that it is safe for a peep along the outside, as explained below.

An Example of Preparation

You are following a car round a long sweeping left bend on a wide two-way road. You anticipate a straight stretch after the corner. Peeping through on the inside of the car in front you have observed that after the third car coming the other way, there will be a gap of at least 30 seconds duration with nothing coming. Fig. 32 (a) shows where you are in the peeping stage, (b) shows where you move up, during the pre-established safe moment for looking along the outside of the car.

From position (b) as the bend opens into the straight you need to be in gear ready to pass quickly, maximising safe use of the straight. If you can't go, you can drop back in, so far as necessary and nothing is lost. Indeed you have gained another pre-view of what is coming and perhaps ascertained how soon you will find a gap, whereas, had

101

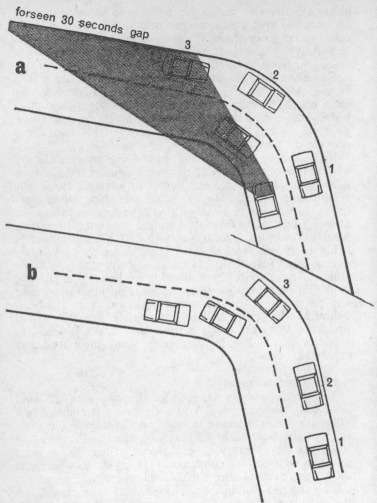

Fig. 32. Overtaking technique.

you waited till after reaching the straight piece, you could easily have found there was now too little of it left in which to overtake safely. The message is get your view early, safely and ready to go or stay.

Sometimes in these circumstances you get a "fastard"

sitting on your tail who you may worry will snooker your "or stay" option. Try flashing your brake lights on and off as this may cure him; if not it is better to drop back and let him leap-frog ahead.

Example of Preparation at Right Hand Curve

In anticipation of the road straightening after a right bend Fig. 33 shows positioning to see ahead and be at the ready. You tuck yourself in near the left hand edge to gain the best view up the straight at the earliest moment. The technique also demands watching lest there is something which may shortly cause the lorry to pull out It is not only concentrating on the road beyond the lorry that matters but watching that the wagon itself will not suddenly have to change direction.

It is seeing through positioning which makes overtaking safer. Then if clear you are positioned to go quickly, before the chance becomes unsafe.

As with looking right and left at junctions the continuing sweeping view counts. You must be sure no hidden vehicle can emerge and cut you off. There may be a dip in the road ahead with cars coming that you cannot see, for example.

What Happens If He Pulls Out?

Even on straight roads and dual carriageways you must be reasonably certain nothing will cause whatever you are overtaking to move out on you. Causes might be rocks, parked cars, often a hidden cyclist, a puddle, wind, anything, including the unbelievable like the driver being stung by a wasp. Experience can lull you into thinking nothing may happen but experience is of little value in unprecedented circumstances! Be on the look-out, with your motoring brain switched on, throughout the manoeuvre. Whenever any vehicle follows another one closely and you come up behind both of them ready to pass, particularly if you have been using the overtaking lane of a dual carriageway and they are on the inside lane for example, it is essential for you to be as certain as possible of the likely behaviour of at least the back driver of the two.

A warning flash from well back and, you may judge a hoot as you get up close may be good driving but must not be allowed to replace dropping your speed down to

103

near his until you are certain that he knows of your intention to pass. If you have been catching up swiftly from a

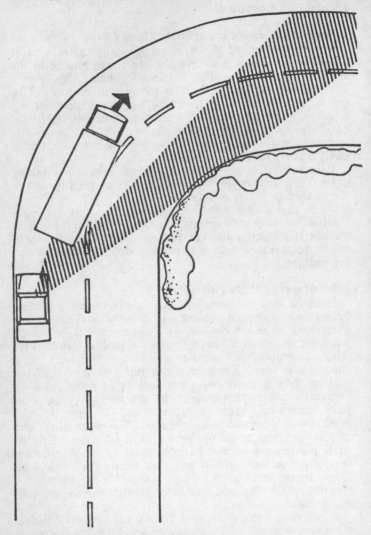

Fig. 33. Preparation for passing.

long way behind you must accept that whether they be deaf, mirror blind, bloody minded, or merely forgetful—the reasons do not matter—it is a fact that some drivers just *do* swing out.

Many bad dual carriageway and motorway smashes result because drivers will not slacken off speed as they rush past bunches of slower traffic. Never be so much faster as you pass that you forfeit the control to avoid a collision if the person you are passing swings out. Remember your *cocoon of safety and swerve margin.*

As you are passing your eyes should range far and near. Just before you commit yourself to pass, a glance at his front wheels can give first warning of his swinging out. Unless he skids, he can hardly come out if his wheels do not turn.

A hoot might be justified if someone did pull out while you were in the act of overtaking but it dare not replace evasive action. Anger is foolish.

WHAT TO DO IF THINGS GO WRONG WHEN YOU ARE COMMITTED TO PASSING AND NEARLY PAST A CAR

Have a game plan ready. Have the car poised and action comes quickly.

"Balance"

At the higher speeds usual for overtaking an emergency swerve (perhaps with hard braking forced upon you as well) could land you in a very frightening skid. To short-circuit this skid potential the secret is to avoid the typical haphazard round detour shown by the dotted path in Fig. 34. Change your style so that you keep the progress of your overtaking generally in straight lines. Fig. 34 shows the correct general principle in plan. The first "straight" line is as you ease out towards position A in Fig. 34, picking up speed while you get up to a position still fractionally behind but outside and parallel to the line of the car you are about to overtake. Between A and B you stay parallel to the car, going straight and accelerating hard, as you safely move up alongside him (the picture cannot allow for the cars moving so I must rely on readers' imagination). At this point you are still not committed. You are still straight and, although hazardous, braking to drop behind should be possible. After B, as you overhaul

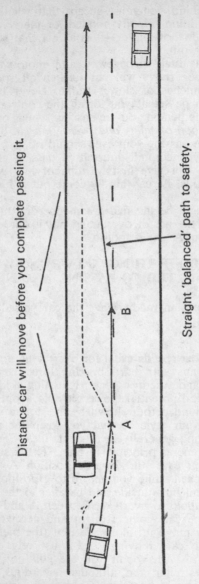

Fig. 34. Passing principle.

the vehicle, it is almost certain you would have to go on because attempting to drop back would be a greater risk. From B the game is to get balanced, going straight, aimed —allowing for the distance the vehicle you are passing will travel in the time (shown projected on Fig. 34)— directly for your safety gap.

B is really the moment from which you are committed to going on, and the important thing from this stage is to have a straight line in your sights to the point where you will be fully back on your own side of the road.

There may be no danger while you are at B. What matters is what may happen in the next split second. Approaching traffic may be coming quicker than you judged or an unruly member may swing out to overtake towards you, or perhaps you will be overtaking on a clear stretch but with a bend looming near when a "fastard" rockets round straight at you or worse skids towards you!

Having set up the straight line from B, then:
a) If no problems arise you simply keep going hard until safely back on your own side.

"DIRECTIONAL CONFIDENCE"

b) Should someone appear round a bend, looming up, even a "fastard", his confidence ought to remain intact. Your deliberate pointing in to the left (you can add left indicator to be *very* advanced) tells him you are already in command of the new situation. He has only to keep well left and judge whether to slow down. If you keep going as you are (straight for safety) it is usually enough and no panic need arise.

Had you been passing in an amateur meandering style, lingering instead of getting on with things, you could in a trice have found yourself having to swing violently to get out of the way, might have skidded, and caused a major accident. Instant fright could confuse the oncomer so that he came on towards you before eventually skidding in an attempt to get clear.

c) In dire emergency on the other hand (e.g. two "fastards" appear one overtaking the other!) you might have to cut in quicker towards your safety gap. Unfortunately the effect has to be to temporarily squeeze the car being passed but life comes first. You must avoid a head-on smash. Being prepared by technique before the danger arose however, your

107

chances of not skidding into the oncoming vehicle are good.

TEXT-BOOKS FRIGHTEN PEOPLE ABOUT CUTTING IN

Many learners are advised never to move in until they can see the whole of the overtaken car in the mirror. Incredible, for it causes people to court peril. Even if you do touch an overtaken car, damage is likely to be slight; compare this with a possible multiple deaths disaster should you hit an approaching car. The silly text-books gloss over that!

Provided the car you pass doesn't have to slow there is no reason for not cutting in as much as you want. It is amazing how close you can go, particularly when your speed is well above his. Glance (rapidly) over your shoulder and see the true facts.

OVERTAKING PRINCIPLE FOR THREE LANE TWO-WAY ROADS

Custom, more than anything makes the rules. You give way to anyone approaching already in the centre lane as he has an equal right to use it.

You should be safe to overtake only if:

1) Nothing is coming (if there is very slow traffic ahead of you overtaking in the centre lane and you have the massive acceleration of a good sports car you might use the outer third lane. The Highway Code, not unreasonably, forbids such use so you would have to be 100% certain that in the particular circumstances the manœuvre was safe—and that you could defend having used it!).

2) Or, when only one vehicle approaches and (a) you have had time to establish nothing follows it which might pull into the middle lane, plus (b) you are 100% certain no-one you are passing might pull out, pushing you without a chance into the oncoming vehicle.

3) Again, once you are sure members of the stream (or the single car) you are passing will not force you out, you should be safe even when several approach in their own left lane provided that none are close behind or catching up each other, thereby being likely to pop out into the middle lane.

108

My advice is, no matter how safe put headlights on and *keep* them on until back to your side.

In (3) above I discard the theory of never being "the meat in the sandwich". I agree with the theory and usually practise it because a pass clear of any approaching traffic is obviously safer. However in the thick traffic nowadays one cannot wait for ever for such a moment. When you do go through the middle, try to be a bit nearer what you are overtaking than to traffic zipping by on the other side. It is a damn sight safer to hit something going your way than it is to hit the chap coming head-on! Irrational though it may be you will notice that some 80% of drivers have not spotted where the balance of safety lies!

FOLLOW MY LEADER OVERTAKING

Once one car moves out to pass, several more often tag on behind, hoping to get by as well. The only safe "tagging" rule is to keep well back from the leading overtaking car, moving in or out by a fraction as required to maintain a *continuous* view of the road ahead. A hoot or a flash for each vehicle you pass is wise as they probably will not expect a second (or third) car to be passing but you must be mindful that in alerting them you are not going to mis-inform the chap in front of you. By keeping slightly off line of the fellow in front any approaching vehicle also *sees you*, a vital safety factor. You can watch whether the gap the man in front chooses will hold you all and still be big enough should the stream further ahead of it brake unpredictably. At all times strive to have a gap ready for emergency retreat. The secret is to keep constant tabs on your options open for room to manoeuvre. If there aren't any, *don't be there*!

Many drivers are unaware of the above safety principles; imagine one such ass "glued" to your tail at speed while you are passing a convoy. Probably the mirror has warned you over the last miles that he is a fool. You must drive accordingly, rejecting any plan you may have had of keeping on passing until the last moment when oncoming traffic has all but arrived, and instead, move into an earlier gap. This leaves the back bumper bumper on his own, facing the oncoming traffic, hopefully with time to get out of the trouble of his own making. You cannot do more for him.

THE WORLD OF DIFFERENCE BETWEEN AN ACCELERATING PASS AND PASSING WITH SPEED IN HAND

When you have to go all out to get by in time, not only may the strain break the engine, you can land in desperate trouble should some vital part such as the accelerator cable snap. Caution insists on a spare safety margin of speed, otherwise never chance it.

On the other hand when you arrive behind with speed in hand (a "flying" pass)—ready to go ahead—and you find all is clear, your ample safety margin can be a little less, because you are not "straining" to get by.

Often by timing arrival at an overtaking point with expert (to an onlooker miraculous) judgement—judgement developed from wary, early, experimental beginnings—you can keep speed going throughout an overtake. You benefit from the safety of speed in hand. For example, when you are arriving from well behind you may have the opportunity to time your arrival behind a car you want to pass to be just the instant a gap develops in the oncoming traffic. *This clear area lets you quickly, softly by.*

With experience, relatively small gaps can be used safely. But, see the next section.

Telling Someone In Front He Should Have The Chance To Pass First

When you catch up a queue held up by something slow the decent thing is to allow earlier arrivals a reasonable chance to pass first. Despite your reaching back marker position all set to pass and probably lying well out, if a car ahead shows readiness and determination to pass the problem, you are morally bound to move in and wait your turn. Moving in tells him via his mirror that you will let him go on first.

If, however, he shows no sign of preparing to go then staying behind him yourself only adds to the jam. Experienced positioning for vision and know-how may enable you to pass safely, when he won't or cannot. You should use it and go then, because every car out of such a queue releases a space for the next arrival behind.

"PRISON"

You are alongside passing a car which is forced out unexpectedly, for example as in Fig. 35, where a child

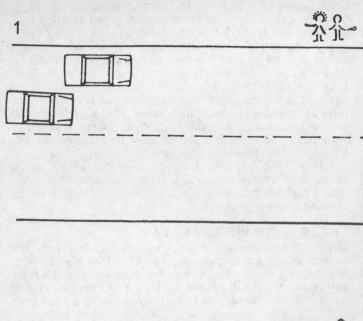

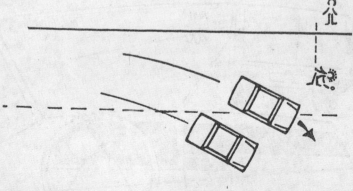

Fig. 35. Action! In emergency.

dashed out because her brother threw her ball on the road. *Giving room to save life is the priority action.* Keep away from the car as much as you can and avoid shutting him in, so he can swing round the child. A split-second emergency may not give time for him to brake. Whether you try to stop or go on (do whichever is safer) is secondary. The main thing is to give the car swerving space. Such action might rebound into another accident depending on traffic flowing the other way or whatever and here your running picture of the traffic scene immediately around you will be crucial in flashing the right course of action to your brain. Sometimes a choice must be made of the less horrific of two potential accidents.

Easily as it happens I have given the above as an example of an overtake which I hope no advanced driver would find himself doing for it is essentially similar to the Russian roulette pass below.

THE RUSSIAN ROULETTE PASS
Despite the remainder of the road being clear only the foolish would try to pass the van ahead in Fig. 36 with approaching cycling children in the distance. The van need only wander slightly (driver looking at scenery, etc.) and those kids are instantly at risk. They probably do not even

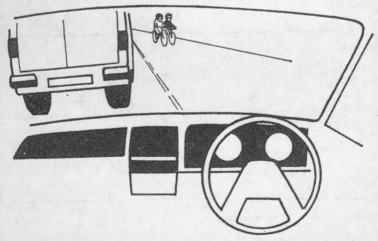

Fig. 36. Never pass here.

see you because cyclists rarely look much above their handlebars, especially the drop variety. In an accident you would be hard put to judge more than 10% of the blame on the van driver, if any; an advanced school would judge you 99% at fault.

6

BAD WEATHER

Using Headlights In Poor Daytime Visibility

Many pundits have tried to attack the law for being too loosely drafted. However all the rule amounts to saying is that in daytime hours if visibility is *seriously reduced*—howsoever caused—it is headlights on while your car is in motion. Daytime means from half-an-hour before sunrise to half-an-hour after sunset. Whenever you are moving means just that. So you cannot switch off just because you are in a queue that happens to be crawling. "Seriously reduced" is the hard one to interpret and here, although the law leaves it to your own judgement in theory, in practice if two policemen swore it was reduced you would be hard put to prove that it was not! However, good law or bad law, good driving says headlights on!

FOG

Speed in fog must be such that you CAN STOP within the distance you can still see.

Use headlights. It is vital to be seen as well as to see and illegal not to wear headlights in poor daytime visibility (see above). Dipped beam, day or night, is usually best. Front fog lamps paired one either side, or a fog lamp and a spot lamp paired and fitted according to the regulations may be used instead of headlights and the extra expense may well be worth it to cut down the back glare. Ideally such lights should be wired so that they cannot come on without your side lights being on otherwise you have nothing alight at the back. Whether or not you find yourself doing enough driving to want to have front fog lights I cannot recommend too highly the extra intensity red rear fog lights which are gradually being fitted as standard equipment. A pair of these can save your life.

In fog, maximum safe speed may be walking pace or

less. Satisfy your conscience that your speed is safe. It takes will-power to resist the temptation to tail someone who whizzes past. He may have superb eyes or lights but he is more probably an idiot.

Following another car and watching its brake lights is very tempting and may seem to make things easier if done from a respectable distance but there is no excuse for crazy close driving. Idiotic "tailing" causes countless pile-ups. And it is probably the chief cause of the multi-storey concertina motorway prang. Perhaps if the police investigated such accidents with more rigour, prosecuting the bad drivers, the word would get around sufficiently to deter some of this mindless driving.

In fog range your eyes ahead, around—also up for traffic lights. Over concentrating on the edge lands you on crossroads before your mind registers. In misty fog, keeping the windows clean is half the battle. Use wipers, and a cloth inside frequently until your demister has the job under full control. Open your windows as fog dampens sound and the "air" keeps you awake! In desperate conditions you may see better by leaning out of the window but if it is that bad why risk your life when you can sleep in the car or stay at a hotel? Park well off the roadway, lights off (if you have to leave it on the side of the road—keep on your own side—and sidelights on). Walk round to satisfy yourself about the safety of your parking position before leaving.

Surprise Patches of Fog

Bewildering, especially at night, these patches are frightening if met at high speed. Unfortunately they are most common through open country, on motorways and on fast roads. It is no good speeding on, hoping a patch is brief; slow instantly, to a crawl if necessary. Re-acceleration later is simple. "Blind" driving is criminal. Remember that the fellow behind (in the mirror) may not appreciate your jamming on the brakes *too* hard.

SPITTING RAIN

Wipers used on a dry screen are quickly damaged, reducing their efficiency. The first sweeps to clear initial rain or spray from cars ahead may stir up dirt and mask vision.

What To Do

    a) Slow down and before you switch on try to choose a

traffic space which will last at least until you can see clearly again. Sometimes you can take the opportunity for that first switch on at traffic lights or similar halts.

b) Use the windscreen washer to clear dirt quickly.

c) Stop the wipers again intermittently so that water builds up and the screen is "washed" as you next switch on. (You may have an intermittent switch feature to do this for you.)

d) Be prepared with a clean windscreen and have a cleansing additive in the washer reservoir containing antifreeze. This gives the wipers a better chance and there is nothing worse in a freeze-up than a squirt which turns directly into ice. (In freezing rain it is essential to have warm air directed at the inside of the screen to prevent instant icing as it settles on the outside.)

e) Look at the road not the drops on the screen.

f) Always carry a clean rag or a leather which you can stop and use if needed.

g) If you do not have a heated rear window a feather mop on a long bamboo cane kept on the back seat enables you to wipe the back window from the driving seat while you wait at traffic lights, etc.

CLOUDBURSTS, TORRENTIAL RAIN

While the worst is on use dipped headlights in order to be seen. Current legislation gives police wide powers to prosecute drivers who do not use headlights in reduced daylight visibility. If passing slower traffic use right indicator as well because these orange repeating lights seem to stick out like sore thumbs, pin-pointing you for oncoming traffic.

Disc brakes may become saturated with water and appear, on application, to have failed for a fleeting but frightening moment before acting. Then they may come on quite fiercely. Initial sweeps by the brake pads on the discs have first to clear the excess water. The manufacturers sometimes advise occasional light pressure on the brake during such conditions to keep the bulk of the water clear.

Another problem is saturation of any type of brake when deep floodwater has been encountered. You must dry the brakes immediately, otherwise they can lose all power. While driving at walking speed, gently hold the brake on with the left foot, driving, as it were, against the brakes, until efficiency returns. Always, after going through any casual water, or a cloudburst, test brakes for loss of efficiency.

OVERTAKING IN RAIN

Increase overtaking margins, I need hardly point out here —by a minimum of three times. Try also to be considerate by keeping well clear as you pass, and avoid lingering in that position from which your wheels directly spray the windscreens of those you have passed.

Next . . .

SUNSHINE

To cheer the reader feeling drenched!

Dazzle in Your Mirror From the Sun

This is a sure sign that if anybody comes the other way they will hardly be able to see you; be ready to hoot and get out of the way. It is astonishing how many drivers still go on when they cannot see for the sun.

When Dazzled Yourself

The best plan is to squeeze the eyelids together seeing through narrow slits and continue slowly enough to be safe. Sun visors help a little when the sun is searing but beware because they allow blinding shots of sunlight past them and also substantially mask the road ahead or to the side.

On really bright days I favour good quality sunglasses or a factory-fitted tinted windscreen even though some of these have recently come under fire in America as a possible cause of accidents because parts of the eye may only be sensitive to light which is being filtered out. The research may be valid but if you have glare-sensitive eyes it is foolhardy to drive any distance without protection. Straining to combat glare induces fatigue and saps the concentration on which life depends. Keep your screen spotless; dirt or greasy marks redouble your problems with glare.

On bright days indicators and brake lights are less visible, and drivers get sleepy, so make allowances for them not seeing your signals—particularly people following if you are turning right off a fast road. Traffic lights and some illuminated road signs can also be very hard to see.

7

NIGHT DRIVING

TWILIGHT OR DAWN, OR POOR LIGHT

You cannot be too early with dipped headlights as dusk approaches. Contrary to misguided opinion this does not wear out your battery; so there is no gain in leaving them off. Indeed the half-light is made treacherous by the many idiots who, not having their headlights on, are scarcely visible. Take extra care, if overtaking, to scan the murk for these gloom merchants.

IN TOWNS

Few would travel in a badly lit street without headlights on but too many drivers still take the view that they are unnecessary in well-lit streets. There may be exceptions but, although you may be able to see without them, the vital thing is you must be *seen*. People leaving side streets tend to look briefly and pull out; they should not, but do. Their glance misses tiny sidelights especially if attention is attracted to a car using headlights, further behind you. *And headlights save pedestrians.* Pinprick sidelights are lost in mirrors.

Helping People At Junctions

At night if a car waits in front of you to join a main road, switching off your headlights reduces glare for him and helps him see his way out. The front driver always needs his appropriate indicator to inform main road drivers and should have headlamps on. If a queue has formed and you are back marker, keep your indicator on to warn new arrivals behind who may then wish to position to filter to one side. Drivers queueing between the front and the back can, as well as dowsing headlamps, keep indicators off to cut down glare, and for the same reason should avoid holding the footbrake on. Wet nights can be Hell when drivers ignore these simple considerations.

When following someone along a well-lit main road who begins to indicate for turning off, you can switch your headlights briefly off and then on again, as well as positioning appropriately, to show them you have the message but never switch off on an unlit road.

MORE TIPS FOR TOWNS AT NIGHT

1) Occasionally you will be leading a stream which meets a handicapped pedestrian or stalled vehicle. Because followers are less likely to see why you are stopping at night it is more essential to stop smoothly leaving a good space between you and the problem. This gives confidence to whoever is in your way; and if bashed from behind, at least there is room for you to be shunted forward.

An early flash of your brake lights warns followers of approaching trouble. Only when absolutely necessary to save lives, stop so positioned that no-one can get past you.

2) At dark junctions, looking right and left needs extra time to sweep across the shadow as distinct from the brightly headlighted patches. The eyes have to adjust. It is your duty to be on your guard for those rare but terrifying darkly-clothed cyclists or kids, perhaps on roller-skates.

3) Usually near schools or big housing estates dare-devil brats sometimes play "last one's a cissy", testing their nerve across your bonnet as they burst from the night shadows. Main roads are their favourites; it pays to scan dark pavements and centre islands at likely times in likely places.

Following Other People

Dip so you do not dazzle. If dazzled yourself slow down. Avoid your eyes dwelling on your wing mirrors and offset the interior mirror by a fraction or use the anti-dazzle feature. These incidentally, give a very different perspective of the scene behind. You need to beware of the feeling of safety brought about by every light behind being dimmed. It gives the impression that people are further behind than they are and tiny lights like cyclists are hard to notice at all. I prefer not to use anti-dazzle in town traffic for this reason.

IN THE COUNTRY

Many are tempted to switch off headlamps when following on unlit country lanes. Don't because:

a) It's illegal.

b) Your width may be wrongly judged by oncomers.

c) Your vision is gravely reduced.

d) The excuse that sidelights prevent dazzling the driver

ahead is irrelevant because if dazzled *he* should go slower. To be considerate, avoid dazzling by dropping further behind.

WHEN LEADING A TRAFFIC STREAM THROUGH COUNTRYSIDE

With nothing ahead and nothing coming, high beam is essential to see properly and as early warning for anyone who comes the other way. Whenever someone comes—dip, returning to high beam as you pass each other if no others appear. If travelling fast towards a corner with no-one in sight, one or two brief up and dip flashes warn anyone who may be coming round it before they appear. The same applies to places like brows of hills where it can be even more important. If tell-tale beams you may already have seen are coming from two cars, one overtaking the other, this alerts them to their folly. People never expect you to be coming fast.

THE PERMANENTLY DIPPED OR "DIPPY" DRIVER

Many lazy (or perhaps fearful) or inexperienced drivers do not bother with high beam at all—and usually they drive just fast enough to make it difficult for anyone to overtake! Passing opportunities are repeatedly lost because people following can only see the length of the slower driver's dipped beam. Growing impatience behind can lead to death risks being taken.

Help faster drivers with high beam; dip once they pass until they are well clear.

Part of the problem may be that the Highway Code fails to give positive advice to the "dippy" about using high beam; however, at least the law does demand that you "retain a full view of the road and traffic ahead". I hope therefore that very advanced drivers will discuss "dippies" far and wide so that the message gets through!

PASSING CYCLISTS OR SMALL OBSTRUCTIONS AT NIGHT

It is doubly important at night to give a right indicator signal in good time briefly, so that followers have warning of somebody or something to be driven round and can allow for it

SPEED IN THE DARK

It is easier to say relate your speed to the area lit than to do it. However, one pedestrian knocked flying because you never saw him in time, perhaps killed. saddens a whole family, not just the selfish driver. Even if the reader feels this is being too emotional I hope he will give honest self-appraisal to his night speeds. Not everyone wears white at night, especially not drunks.

Go more slowly on high beam than in daytime, and when dipped, more slowly still.

Dazzling

If dazzled you must slow or stop till you can see. Do not take risks or blame others; reduce dazzle by concentrating on seeing your side of the road rather than allowing the eyes to be "hypnotised" by approaching beams.

A brief up flash reminds an approaching driver to dip, but deliberately dazzling back is childish, increasing danger. Always dip before junctions or roundabouts because there frequently isn't time later.

On empty main roads flashing lights up and down, even if there is no apparent approaching traffic, announces your presence at hazards. In the seconds you are dipped you see approaching light beams easily. In the seconds you are on full beam others see yours.

In addition to the advice given under "Helping People at Junctions", in traffic streams you can use your judgement to cut braking applications to a minimum, saving brake light glare for those behind.

OVERTAKING AT NIGHT

I suggest that there are no circumstances where overtaking without headlights on makes any sense. Even on a brilliantly lit suburban dual carriageway it is essential that the person you are overtaking has every chance of knowing you are coming past.

Similarly on three-lane two-way roads do not be lulled into a false sense of security—keep your headlights on—and not just when you use a middle lane to overtake!

In situations like the above two, high beam at any stage of an overtake may be inappropriate with the danger of dazzling drivers going the other way. However, for example, out of town, where overtaking normally involves no oncoming traffic, a brief up flash of your headlights alerts initially that you hope to be coming by; you only switch to continuous high beam for full ahead vision once you are alongside, when doing so can no longer dazzle the chap you are passing. As you raise your beam and shortly slip in front he can courteously dip his beam.

A Passing Headache

How do you pass a "dippy" (page 119)? Lie well out when safe. Put on high beam before you begin to overtake, long enough to establish all will be clear. Beware of dazzling him via his mirror which would be illegal, and might make him hit the brakes or wander. If time and vision allow, revert to low beam until you get up alongside. This can be the only way to see far enough ahead for a safe pass.

Extra Risks Overtaking At Night

Distances are harder to judge at night. Suppose you are overtaking and not quite ready to move back in when a car approaches round the next corner. The approaching driver may not grasp straightaway that you are on his side. All he sees are two sets of headlamps with little speed differential or other guiding factor to tell by. When he realises the truth he may panic.

To defuse this potential panic you need to get quickly back into your own side and *to be seen getting in*. If time and safe, brake and fall in behind. If not, instant left flasher warns that you are being forced to cut into your own side which ought to be less of a worry than a possible head-on smash. The driver you are passing may be expecting it and be braking already. Strangely, drivers seem to be less aggressive at night; so he is less likely to accelerate piggishly. A rapid glance over your shoulder may well show you could move in sooner than you thought.

Signals For Night-Time Overtaking

At night a brief right wink during the early moving out stage makes it easier for following drivers (perhaps with poorer night eyes) to pick out just what you are doing ahead. You may judge that it is better to keep it on during the overtaking, depending on circumstances. The orange repeating lamp is distinct and, in addition to headlamps, will stand out from a longer way ahead.

DIM HEADLAMPS
Keep outside headlamp glass clean; on motorways especially, even a few hundred yards of filthy conditions can leave you wondering if headlights are really on! Never drive if one headlight has failed; you may be mistaken for a motorbike!

8

MOTORWAY DRIVING

WHICH LANE?
On three-lane carriageways the Highway Code rules you stay in lane 1, numbering from the left, if 1 is full—2, and for passing only—3. The fast driver in lane 3 may consider my "proviso" on page 36 applicable here too. However it can be no excuse for hogging the outside lane at the maximum speed limit when people want to pass. Such drivers can and should be prosecuted for obstruction as explained in Chapter 3.

Drivers who dream along in lane 2, oblivious of room to move back to lane 1, are in my view the root cause of bunching—the big motorway killer. If a few such dreams were shattered in Court, our M-ways would be a lot safer. By filling the middle lane these drivers provide an excuse for lane 3 obstructors; they reduce the degree of separation of fast and slow traffic; and they foster under-passing.

For example, bunching hits lane 1 whenever speeds have to fall to avoid under-passing of these lane 2 dream-alongs. Lane 1 lorries and others, formerly close to their best turn of speed, then have to move out to maintain that speed past slower stuff. Because of the long distances needed to edge ahead again, lengthy bunching soon backs up behind them. A few dream-alongs caught up in that, soon wake up and shift to lane 3, swiftly slowing that lane down to their level. Lane 3—already overloaded with obstructors who should be in lane 2 1 (page 88)—then rapidly bunches too. The result is the familiar too-close driving of which multiple accidents are made.

DO NOT FOLLOW DIRECTLY
It is especially in these baulked conditions that the very advanced driver constantly *adjusts* his "thinking and stopping" gap. As the motorway curves it may get shorter if

forward vision improves. On a straight stretch it must lengthen, and he will often make use of a fractional move sideways relative to the line of traffic ahead in his lane, never sharply, better to command the far ahead view. The scope for this movement is dictated by traffic behind and alongside but "never follow the wheel tracks" is his motto for avoiding the unexpected jam-on braking which so often ensnares the less cautious. It is part of keeping a "cocoon" of safety about you. Being off-track of the man ahead, even a fraction, gives you the chance to see out ahead and anticipate trouble. When there is an emergency like a fallen exhaust pipe on the road it puts you one jump ahead.

Another visual art on motorways, especially in bad conditions and at night, is to pan your eyes constantly upstream ahead looking for any breaks in the flow of the traffic. You can often check the flow all the way to the horizon but it is the *flow* (rather than individual vehicles in the stream) in the immediate quarter to half mile ahead that matters. Immediately that flow falters you can begin easing off, probably well before many of those ahead of you spot the problem.

MOTORWAY MIRRORS
Never trust your first mirror sighting. Unless you assess the speed of a passer with several checks over time, you cannot judge how quickly he is catching you. Even then, I advise a glance over your right shoulder before moving out. It is the most certain way to spot that fellow shadowing your back wing, the one who "cannot be there"... but is!

RIGHT INDICATOR FOR OVERTAKING
Moving from lane 1 to lane 2 an unexpected party may need your right indicator—a lane 3 driver who decides to move to lane 2 at just the same moment! Even with your indicator, that glance across your shoulder can be the saver that stops you slapping into him. Conversely, whenever you return to lane 2 from 3, left indicator and a glance over that shoulder are prerequisites. The dreaded under-passer (described earlier) will also be needing your left signal and glance. Hold your finger on the control so you cannot forget to cancel it. Where slip roads join, similar considerations apply to moving onto or getting back to lane 1.

As part of their professional code lorry drivers sometimes give a single blink with their right indicator which can confuse the car driver who may be about to overtake. The signal is a "thank you" by the lorry driver in the middle lane to another lorry driver in the inside lane who has just flashed his headlights to let the first one know that he is now far enough ahead to move in safely. It means: "Thank you for telling me I may move in, however I have decided to stay in this lane and go on until I overtake the next vehicle ahead." The thank you for the headlight flash, when he *does* move in, is a touch of his brake lights.

SPEED BOGGLING
After several hours 70 m.p.h. can feel like 30 m.p.h. Always check your speedometer as you leave a motorway. Counter the illusory effects with a regular schedule of rest stops. Part cause is fatigue, the killer which the discipline of fresh-air-stops helps combat.

DROWSINESS
If you feel sleepy before you can exit a motorway I suggest you open your window, pinch yourself, sing, whistle, etc. but pull up on the hard shoulder if you cannot make it safely to an exit.

LANE DISCIPLINE
Suppose you are in lane 2. A driver, concerned about traffic merging onto the motorway, pulls out from the nearside lane regardless of you. NEVER swing out, slap in front of fast-lane traffic. That is how multi-storey accidents are caused. Slow up: *keep in lane*. The advanced driver expands his gap in front before access link slip-ways, and/or shifts to lane 3 in advance, subject to other traffic. He also takes a special refresher of the mirror picture.

After a skilful merge into busy left-lane traffic from an access slip-way you can help middle-lane traffic already bearing down to pass you, to do so in safety. Just a couple of left winks (no more) "promises" them you will hold the left lane till they are passed.

MOTORWAYS IN BAD WEATHER
Beware of fog patches (see page 114). In a "pea-souper" I am bound to suggest that you do not go on the motorway. Heavy lorries are advised to keep to the left lane in fog and generally they do. Other traffic is advised in turn to stay out of the left lane.

Driving into a fog blanket there can be times with no one in sight ahead, which make it almost impossible to quantify the distance clear of problems in front of you. Some measure of that distance can sometimes be gained by reference to oncoming headlights on the opposite carriageway, if perchance there is a constant stream over there. The point at which they are emerging from the gloom can be related distance-wise to the fogged area in front of you. Up to the distance those headlights are coming into view you can be moderately sure that anything with lights on ahead of you would be visible. This is no 100% fog driving panacea—so never depend on it alone.

In high winds grip the steering wheel firmly, especially going over and under bridges, as you pass high-sided vehicles, etc. If the roads are wet a gust of wind can literally sweep your car sideways pushing it several feet across the road in a skid. Get your speed down if you want to survive and keep a cool nerve!

Never exceed 70 m.p.h. on wet (see page 130). Clear disc brakes of water frequently (see page 115). In dense traffic on the motorway there is so much spray during heavy rain headlights become essential. Although the *general* "daytime visibility" may not be "seriously reduced", the endless convoys of lorries produce such vast fields of spray that it becomes partially so. In the mirror, where it so often counts on the motorway, people simply will not see you without headlights on.

During maintenance, contra-flow diversions often place the two opposite direction fast lanes in direct proximity, separated only by red and white striped poles. Statistics reveal appalling accident rates for such lanes. Except in perfect weather and daylight, therefore, I always stay out of them given a choice.

Snow—Black (Invisible) Ice

The skidding chapter, 10, discusses black ice. The vast snowdrift, untouched by gritter or snowplough, can be very frightening. Traffic melts most falling snow but sometimes in isolated places, a snowdrift abruptly funnels three lanes into one! At night you come upon it in a split second with no warning. Remember in squally, snowy weather it only wants one drift in a whole motorway to land you in a pile-up.

MOTORWAY ACCIDENTS

A recent straw poll amongst motorway police which I conducted threw up, based on gut feeling, the four most common causes of fatalities on our motorways. They were *driving too close to the vehicle ahead, fatigue*, tyre failure, and shed loads.

The finding that driving too close is one chief cause supports much of what has been said in this book. Fatigue in my view has far more to do with accidents than drink; we cannot measure it but very advanced drivers can spread the word and encourage people to be realistic about whether they should drive or sleep. See Chapter 12 about burst tyres. Most manufacturers recommend a few extra pounds for sustained high speed; consult your car's book of words. The extra pressure counteracts flexing and heat, a tyre's worst enemy. The Highway Code urges you to use the roadside telephone and inform the police should you come upon any debris lying on the motorway causing danger, or should something fall from your own vehicle. It suggests that you do not try to retrieve it yourself. If you keep an eye out and you see another vehicle which is about to lose its load, whilst the driver may be unaware, the thing to do is to call up the police on the nearest telephone so that they can pull the vehicle in and save a very nasty accident.

If you get into a smash but happily are unhurt remember that unless all lanes are blocked other traffic will pound relentlessly on, probably at 70 m.p.h. Hence minor incidents turn fatal. And "rubbernecks"—who practically stop to gape—have even caused pile-ups on the opposite carriageway! If you cannot help, keep going, out of the way.

Those involved must shelter the injured from speedsters while help is summoned. Get hazard warning lights on. Raise your bootlid or tailgate to indicate distress. At night keep tail-lamps on. If you have one and traffic allows, set up a red safety triangle at least 150 metres back. Otherwise I suggest you stand it on your car roof. Switch off all ignitions and put out all cigarettes, to avert fire.

Check casualties for breathing—you may have to attempt the kiss of life immediately. Support the head if need be to ensure the person's windpipe is clear. Arrest bleeding if you can. Offer no drink. Reassure and stay with anyone injured. In the absence of medical knowledge cover the hurt with clothing or rugs for warmth but unless they are at risk from passing traffic do not attempt to move them. Able-bodied victims may be safest up (or down) the bank off the motorway entirely—children and animals under control—depending whether all traffic has stopped and on the relative safety of getting them there.

If possible without risk to more traffic or the injured, move driveable vehicles onto the hard-shoulder. However, unless *all* vehicles can be shifted it may be safer to await emergency recovery, than to "open" a dangerously narrowed carriageway.

"Tail-back duty" is the police expression for warning drivers that there is an accident up ahead. Some forces regard this duty as so important they even place it a shade higher in their priorities than getting another squad car to the scene of the accident itself. If you suddenly see a huge queue up ahead, making it obvious there has been an accident, and you find yourself ploughing to a halt, I strongly recommend switching on your four-way hazard warning lights well before you come to a stop—especially if you are concerned that people behind have not yet seen what you have seen. Technically use of four-way flashers on the move is illegal but for me staying alive counts! I might even switch red extra-intensity rear fog lights on and off to shout the message louder until I saw people behind had got it. In stopping for such a hold-up I would always leave a car length or two ahead of me initially so that if the chap behind were to threaten careering into the back of me in his skidding attempt to stop I would have a few yards free to move forward, possibly saving the day. I would be ready ultimately to get my head down below the level of the top of the seat-back and tell my passengers so that all the heads could be saved from whiplash, the neck breaker.

THE "PSYCHO" FLASH
Faster drivers are often baulked by slowsters blocking the overtaking outside lane. Once you come behind one, no amount of light flashing persuades him to move over. A "psycho" flash given much earlier, from a long way behind however, can make the slowster think you are coming much faster than you are and "psyche" him into moving over. Never do it to somebody making the proper use of the outside lane with other traffic to overtake.

Where a high speed queue builds up behind an obstructive lane 3 hog you often find the first few behind him do not flash any request to move over, nor do they pull over themselves. You can be stuck for ages. A way round this is to wait for a curve in the motorway at which (traffic in the other direction permitting at night) a strategic measured headlight flash from you will reach the leading driver's mirror.

9

AUTOMATIC TRANSMISSION

ONLY THE RIGHT FOOT
This rule prevents all mistakes.

Reverse With The Right Foot
Feather-light control for manoeuvring is designed in. Gentle accelerator use gains it. Hold the brake with the right foot as you swap between drive and reverse.

Check Your Advanced (Correct) Moving Off Procedure
1) Apply footbrake (right foot).
2) Select drive, release handbrake.
3) Hold car with footbrake, check it is safe to go.
4) If safe, right foot moves to accelerator.

Advanced Hill Starting Off
Release handbrake instead of at (2) above, at (4) above, after slight acceleration makes the car strain to go.

Traffic Queues
When stopped with handbrake on, select neutral to prevent "creep" against the handbrake.

Pitfalls For Those Who Have To Chop And Change Between Manual And Automatic Cars
Going to manual, you may forget to put the clutch down. Going to automatic, it is the very thing you remember! You find yourself jamming on the brakes! Watch out!

10
SKIDDING

Probably 98% of skidding accidents arise unexpectedly through ignorance. Prevention through anticipation is the life-saver to learn for they are much harder to correct than to avoid.

CAN YOU CONTROL SKIDS?
Sometimes corrective action eases a skid and enables an earlier return to control but because time and space to act are so often absent, escapes from severe skids without accident are usually luck.

THREE MAIN TYPES OF SKID
SKIDS WHEN BRAKING HARD
OVER-ACCELERATION SKIDS
THE DEADLY SIDESLIP SKID. (Where the whole car appears to slide bodily. It may be a front (or steering) wheel skid alone that gives this impression or all wheels, although apparently rolling forward at speed, may drift, skidding or sliding off the steered course, sometimes called a four-wheel drift.)

Each type has similar causes:
a) Mechanical defect in the car.
b) A road cause.
c) Human error.

After a skid has happened you usually find a combination of (a) plus (c), (b) plus (c), or all three caused the trouble. The hardest to admit although strongest element 98 times out of 100 is (c).

DEFINITION OF TERMS
Locked Brakes
"Locking" means when a wheel or wheels stop rolling; momentum (weight x speed) thereafter carries the car along with that (or those) wheel(s) sliding.

Aquaplaning
On wet roads, traction (road grip) gradually lessens as speed rises until the tyres, instead of gripping, are sculling on a film of water. Fig. 37 shows this, greatly magnified.

Fig. 37. Aquaplaning.

It has been proved that with rear wheel drive a front wheel can actually stop revolving as it starts to aquaplane. With front wheel drive, immediately the film of water intervenes and direct contact between the tyre and the road is lost you can get wheelspin, even at 60 m.p.h. or less. The frightening thing is, in both types, once the front wheels aquaplane—all steering control vanishes.

As a water skier will skim the surface at speed but sink when he stops, so cars "ski" and "sink". In all types of car (sports cars are no more immune than others) aquaplaning on a damp surface can set in from about 65 m.p.h. to 70 m.p.h. but less if tyres or road surface are bad. Luck shows no mercy if you exceed this borderline speed on wet roads.

Do not be fooled that such a speed will always be safe. On a straight open road empty of traffic with no cross-wind and no likelihood of being forced to swerve or stop quickly, perhaps; but, if there is other traffic or any possibility of having to brake, no! Your "cocoon" of safety must be greatly enlarged. Your "stopping and thinking" gap has to be extended to counteract the possibility of locked brake aquaplaning explained below.

On wet roads up to about 70 m.p.h. good tread can cope with considerable road surface water by squelching it out behind and, depending on design, a certain amount is squeezed away to the sides. If there was no space for the water (as with bald tyres) science could probably prove aquaplaning would commence at about 30 m.p.h. The area of tread which actually contacts the road at any given moment is only about the size of the sole of a man's shoe.

The tread works its "magic" by the revolving of the wheel bringing a constant fresh supply of "thirsty" tread. As each area of tread meets the road surface (A, Fig. 38) it mops up the loose surface water. This it stores during the fraction of a second before again leaving the tarmac (B, Fig. 38) when it sprays it out behind.

UNDER 65—70 M.P.H.

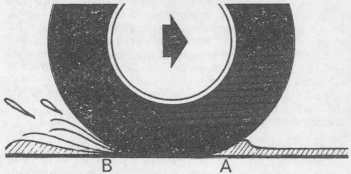

Fig. 38. How a tyre clears water.

Locked Brake Aquaplaning

If you lock brakes on wet roads the tread is robbed of its mechanism for clearing away the water. The locked wheel(s) will tend to aquaplane until again allowed to rotate. They can continue to "ski" down to 10 m.p.h.— 5 m.p.h. or less, if stuck locked. What happens is the water, now a "torrent" because it can't get away, works like a continuous "wedge" into the angle between the tread (in front) and the road. This lifts the wheel into aquaplaning. While aquaplaning continues there is almost no effective stopping of the car and you have no steering control.

SKIDS WHEN BRAKING HARD

Page 133 charts typical (a), (b), (c) causes (see page 129), which can combine, starting these skids.

Prevent These Hard Braking Skids

Keep the car in top mechanical condition. It is false

131

economy and death-courting to use worn tyres. Check air weekly. Brakes must have attention at the manufacturers' specified intervals.

At safe places check the treacherousness of any doubtful surfaces by testing. (See "Road Causes" in the chart, page 133.) Start test braking at crawling speeds, increasing your experience with extreme caution, a little at a time, when roads are empty and no-one could get into a bump. This is how advanced drivers are made!

The experienced maintain vigilance on all changing road surfaces. Suspect surfaces are always treated with respectful caution, speed being dropped until a test confirms it can safely be increased. If gradual icing is feared, for example at night, tests may be required every few minutes or wherever the road crosses an area exposed to the wind and chill. You must know the condition of the surface at all times.

Test brakes under any extra load so that you appreciate the vast additional stopping distances required and the increased possibility of losing balance and control.

Spotting A Mechanical Fault

Slow punctures can be detected by heavier steering or other uncharacteristic response to your steering, perhaps along with bumping noises. Wrongly adjusted brakes usually pull a car to one side, progressively more so with rising speeds.

It may be useless only to test a brake system at 30 m.p.h. It is often only at 65 m.p.h. to 70 m.p.h. on dry roads (test gingerly to start with) that a fault is sufficiently magnified for early detection.

I have made a brake test at 45 m.p.h. and the brakes appeared normal; yet, in the same conditions, when absolutely safe to do so, I have found the car is swung to one or other side by a test at 70 m.p.h. This was the only early indication the brakes needed repair. Know your brake power!

ON WET, INCREASE YOUR "STOPPING AND THINKING" GAP THREE TIMES MINIMUM; ON ICE, TENFOLD MAY NOT BE ENOUGH.

A 200-yard skid is by no means impossible.

SKIDS WHEN BRAKING HARD

Wheel(s) lock(s) up. Car slides forward, may lose sideways control and begin to spin round or all steering may be lost if (on a wet road) Locked Brake (front wheel) Aquaplaning occurs. Results are exaggerated if the steering is in lock (e.g. turning for a bend), or if braking on a corner or adverse camber and on downhills, or when extra loads are carried.

Likely

CONTRIBUTORY CAUSES

(a) MECHANICAL DEFECTS

Treadless tyre(s). Soft or over-inflated tyres. Slow puncture. Front wheels (or rear) not having tyres of matching tread pattern, **condition** or type (e.g. radials illegally mixed with cross ply). Over-loading. Lopsided load. Wrongly adjusted brakes. Poor suspension-particularly shock absorbers (which dampen up and down reaction of the springs at bumps). Other more technical defects causing "locking".

(b) ROAD CAUSES

Wet surface (raining or not). Slippery surface (oil etc.). Mixed surfaces having different anti-skid properties. Cobbles shiny, or wet. Loose surfaces (gravel, wet leaves, mud etc). Uneven surface. Black (invisible) ice or "freezing" rain, Slush, Ice/Snow.

(c) HUMAN ERRORS

Sudden stabbed instead of progressive braking. Excessive braking pressure by driver. Human error in not making allowances for (a) and/or (b) or having sufficient regard for exaggerating factors (see above) is the chief reason for these skids. Advanced drivers anticipate and almost never skid un-wittingly. They know the terror and drive to avoid skids.

133

How To Deal With Hard Braking Skids

1) Steer straight or as straight as possible instantly. Turned steering encourages brake locking and getting your car into a spin.

In the fastest stop, the wheels at no time lock but are braked to the point of locking throughout. The retarding effect depends solely on tyre grip. The constant supply of fresh tread, maintained by keeping the wheel rolling, is therefore crucial.

Directly a wheel locks, one small pad of tread has all the work to do and no hope of retarding as effectively. This tiny area of tread abruptly finds itself scraping along the abrasive surface leaving a trail of skid rubber. It heats rapidly, and may even start to melt. Worse on wet roads, it may simply aquaplane instead (see page 129).

To apply precisely the hardest possible pedal pressure that will still not quite lock the brakes needs either a genius or some sort of computer-aided sensor device. A very few cars are now being fitted with such a device but it is early days to forecast their widespread adoption due to their cost and sophistication. Owners of such machinery are well-placed in emergency but need to be mindful that other people cannot stop so quickly.

2) For everyone else, in practice, in emergency you press firmly (if need, rapidly increasing the pressure until quite hard) to the point where a wheel does lock, instantly easing a fraction when this happens, so as to unlock. Equally instantaneously, for a locked wheel generally releases within a split second of your easing, back on with resolute pressure to the lock point ready to ease—only ease note— coming back with firm pressure the same as before instantly it unlocks again. By repetition you strive towards the ideal that will stop you fastest—holding the brakes on the point of locking throughout.

You will find progressively harder pedal pressures can be applied without locking as your speed drops to a halt. Your rapid on . . . ease . . . and instantly on again process, to ensure your braking is as near as possible to the locking point at every stage, automatically makes certain you apply this mounting pressure as a stop is reached.

As 1) above tells, whenever braking fiercely, steer as straight as possible. Directional stability returns mostly during the seconds brake pressure is eased, but drive to straighten immediately and continue to.

If you insensitively lock the brakes for long, not only do you not stop as effectively as possible, you may get into danger of the car beginning to spin. Once she starts to turn—your warning—the dramatic abruptness with which you can find yourself spinning more, going backwards, or crashed, is terrifying.

Should you sense the back begin to slide to one side or the other, or in popular jargon "to overtake the front", you need to react niftily and steer that same way; as the motto has it, "steer into the skid". Left, if the back slides left, right, if right; with luck this. *combined with* easing the brakes, will stop the spin in time, allowing you to restore heavy braking with your steering straight.

An Extremely Rare Occurrence

You are desperately trying to stop but control disappears from the front of the car. No response comes from the steering; no amount of easing the brake seems to unlock the front wheels. You may not have noticed greasiness or ice as the cause, or on wet roads, it could be locked brake aquaplaning (see page 131). In this apparently hopeless situation a sharp hard—on—off handbrake jab sometimes induces the back to slide or in some way alters the balance of the car and steering response returns. The breath of control regained allows you to steer to safety and re-harness your brakes.

So Far We Have Looked Mainly At Theory

What happens when you are skidding and faced with "piling" into stopped traffic?

Answers

1) If there is a clear pavement, or room to the right without head-on danger, steer for it! (Note: mirror knowledge might reject this move.) You might have to ease braking substantially initially to get the steering response required.

2) Hoot and flash! Stopped traffic might realise and be able to move forward; anyway it warns them to expect you and to try to avert neck damage (see page 127).

Thinking ahead as regards 1) above, the advanced driver is continually planning, during the sort of traffic conditions which tend to be punctuated with sudden stops, where his escape routes could be in the event. His mind

Fig. 39. Avoiding a direct killer smash.

works subconsciously away so that if a stop happens, as a passenger you suddenly appreciate that he has "manufactured" a stopping or avoiding distance out of "nowhere". Though quite close behind traffic from time to time, he always has his alternatives lined up.

An Amazing Skid

A friend, tootling through a town at 30 m.p.h., was suddenly confronted by a long lorry which shot across his bows from a building entrance, shown by Fig. 39. He realised he had no chance of stopping in a straight line.

Knowing there was no-one coming the other way he endeavoured to avoid a smash by steering right, deliberately swinging on to the arc shown by the arrows which lengthened his space for stopping. This more than compensated for the more difficult "braking on the turn". From about half-way round his wheels actually locked and the car slid bodily sideways towards the lorry.

He finished up parallel to the side of the lorry, only two inches away, but even had he hit it the accident would have been unlikely to injure as he had by then slowed so much and the whole side of the car was ready to take the load of a crash.

While the car slid bodily towards the lorry in the last few seconds with all wheels locked, the edges of the tyres probably did the last bit of sideways stopping by "scraping", dragging across the road surface.

The action taken was possibly the only one which could have worked to avoid a crash. Unfortunately such evasive action cannot always be taken because of other traffic and it would seem a doubtful option at any higher speed. I describe it because it happened rather than in recommendation.

MORE ABOUT SURFACES
You can find basic facts in the chart on page 133.

Wet
On wet surfaces, brake locking starts more easily and earlier than on dry. Required stopping distances are dramatically increased. Cut speed generally by one-third at least; also multiply your "stopping gap" three times or more.

Traffic Dust, Oil And Wet
Anyone whose home is near a busy highway will know how much muck and dust is created which seeps through their windows and doors. This film of dust which is a constant feature of any road can become lethal when it gets wet and all mixed up, together probably with a few oil droppings, and flecks of tyre rubber. Particularly if there has only been a shower or while heavy rain has only been on for half-an-hour or so, this invisible mixture seems to spread rapidly into wide areas of "banana skin" conditions. Black ice can seem friendly by comparison! Traffic lights and corners seem to be very susceptible. Only heavy rain for a good long time seems to wash the slipperiness away. Damp patches left on otherwise dry roads are real traps because you tend to come on them at fast speeds.

When you hit a surface like this even feather-light braking may lock the wheels; the tyres cannot grip and just slide. Fortunately, apart from being aware that conditions may be ripe for such a slippery patch, a feeling of lightness or a slight over-acceleration skid may warn you. *Accept any such warning as a major alert.*

Loose Surfaces (Gravel, Wet Leaves, Mud, Etc.)
Your tyres grip the leaves, mud, etc., but these slide over the road; I only hope your first experience of this will not be the last!

Black (Invisible) Ice ... The Surprise Killer

In winter, weight of traffic, gritting and salt usually keeps most important roads usable. Overnight frost is quickly melted in the sun to a damp surface. It is worth being aware this is skiddier—because of the salt content—than pure wet. However, major problems are then diminished (*except* in shaded places where ice or part-ice may remain for longer—look out for patches that have not been beaten by the traffic) until the late afternoon/evening when the "black" ice begins to form again. How can you tell just when and where the damp turns to ice?

Two ways: *By ear*... Through a slightly open window you can hear the characteristic hiss of the tyres on a damp or wet surface. On ice all is quiet, deathly silent. The contrast is your immediate warning. You still need to be cagey though because sometimes even with the hiss the ice has not melted right through to the road. You are running on water but it is still on top of ice! *By tyre-watching*... It may be possible to get quick glances at the tyres of other vehicles. Once the ice is melting you can see the tell-tale spray being thrown up, particularly on sunny, frosty days.

Ice nearly always identifies itself by lightness of the steering—or a slight, unexpected tail waggle—a general uncertain feeling in the way the car is responding to the controls. Expect such signs in wintry conditions. Take the hint if you see lorry or other professional drivers going slowly, or motorcyclists taking to their feet, or if ice is forming on parked cars. Much over 15 m.p.h. or 20 m.p.h. on black ice is extremely risky; usually you must be going slower. "Freezing rain", as weathermen call it, is very similar and in minutes the road can turn so glassy that driving becomes practically impossible. Be very careful if you are driving out of town on a cold morning. There may be no sign of ice in the town but when you get into the country you can find that whereas everybody else is fully aware of the ice, you are the only one who has not spotted it! It may only surprise you the once.

Snow Or Snow With Ice On Top

From the braking point of view snow is nasty; iced over as well it may be diabolical. For normal stopping use gentle braking.

If even a touch on the brakes locks the wheels, drop down the gears until she grinds to a halt in first, using engine compression control. Note that the slight jerk as you let in the clutch with each lower gear may lock the driving wheels if you do not match road to engine speed fairly accurately. (See how to double de-clutch, page 30.)

So slippery can conditions become that, even at walking speed, just turning the steering for a corner is sufficient for the wheels to lock and slide you straight on.

At under 10 m.p.h. on snow you can sometimes use this fact, that she will go straight with the wheels turned, as a last ditch help in stopping (if you will excuse the expression)! While continuing to brake very gently, swing rapidly on to full lock so that in effect you present the edge of the tyre widthways to "scrape" at the snow. If it begins to turn spin over to the other lock. The success of the technique (for which there is rarely much time) depends on how compacted the snow is. It is better on loose snow and probably its chief use is for stopping again, when you have tested the first few yards of a steep hill down, found it was too jolly steep to continue, but have no wish to career on down and have no other means to stop!

If you must drive in such lethal conditions make use, where it is in your favour, of the camber of the road. While no-one can guarantee to control a skidding vehicle the very advanced, by keeping the camber on their side, can at least, usually, skid in a safer direction. Even an inch on to the wrong camber can throw you into an accident skid—perhaps instead of a relatively harmless slide into the near-side grass verge.

When snow and ice come, take the opportunity to study the effect that road camber has on skidding, on an isolated road. Discover in safety how to relate your driving to the camber. Find out how much better it is to get on to fresh snow near the edge, where the tyres bite better. At hills always stop or drop to a snail's pace at the top to assess the situation before descending. It is too late half-way down. Depending on traffic, on severely-cambered roads it pays to keep near to the middle on the hill, so that on braking any slide does not take you straight into the gutter. In real danger bumping the edge or aiming for a snowdrift could be better than careering down.

I have known a hill become so slippery that when I tried to stop at the top before going down I could not! She slid on and on, although quite slowly at first. I therefore took reverse gear and gently began to spin the driving wheels

139

backwards. Like "magic" this measurably checked my speed, already gathering with the steepness of the hill. Although too much reverse wheelspin started to turn the car and had to be reduced, I was still able to control speed enough to reach the bottom safely. Flashing my headlights was fortunately sufficient to warn the people waiting at the bottom that I could scarcely stop.

OVER-ACCELERATION SKIDS

This category has similar (a), (b), (c) causes which are charted on page 141.

Control of these acceleration "wheelspin" skids as they are often termed is normally simple if their cause is understood and they are sensed quickly. The skids happen when starting from rest and, with more ferocious results, if accelerating too harshly from one speed to a higher speed. Judgement of surfaces and controlled acceleration are the chief weapons of prevention.

Starting From Rest

A surface may be so slippery that moving off is impossible without some wheelspin. The secret is to use the highest gear that will just take the car away without stalling and to almost stall in the process. This minimises wheelspin.

On snow the game is to get this right first time or the wheel very quickly becomes dug in. Keep the front wheels straight or you make it harder. The very advanced part of the game is not to stop in the first place where you might get stuck! Every trick of timing is employed to avoid complete stops on uphills or against the camber. Parking is only risked in favourable spots.

If you do get stuck it is worth knowing that spinning the wheels in an effort to move off on snow, wears tread away almost as fast as it melts the snow! If a wheel has dug itself in and you have tried all the tricks helpful bystanders urge, like "rocking" forwards and backwards, in (hopefully) bigger and bigger sweeps, try turning off the engine, leaving her in neutral and simply push the car out of the hole. It works! The same applies on mud. When either condition is likely it is worthwhile carrying a spade.

Once you are on the move, if traction is not 100% or the driving wheels' end of the car slides sideways, it will be because wheelspinning is still excessive. Directly you

OVER-ACCELERATION SKIDS

One or both driving wheels spin and only slightly grip or fail to grip the road to move the car. There may be loss of sideways control at the driving end as well. (Be it rear wheel drive or front wheel drive.)

Likely

CONTRIBUTORY CAUSES

(a) MECHANICAL DEFECTS

Soft or over-inflated tyres. Slow puncture. Treadless tyres on one or both driving wheels. Overloading or lopsided loading. Other obscure defect.

(b) ROAD CAUSES

Wet surface. Slippery surface (grease, oil, etc.). Mixed surfaces having different anti-skid properties. Cobbles shiny, or wet. Black ice/Freezing rain. Snow/Ice on top of snow. Adverse camber may accentuate loss of sideways control.

(c) HUMAN ERRORS

Ferocious acceleration in lower gears or jerky acceleration. As above when on a bend or corner makes a skid more likely. Using too low a gear. Human error in allowing for (a) and (b) lets these skids happen.

reduce this wheelspinning by easing acceleration (just enough will do) steering control and normal forward motion should return.

Uphills In Snow

Short uphills are tackled with a cautious build-up of speed (after waiting for any drivers ahead to clear) in order to keep going in the highest possible gear; longer hills are best tackled from the bottom in the gear that will get you to the top and beyond because the chances are if you have to change, wheelspin may defeat further progress directly your clutch comes up. If you have to change down, do so with confidence, quickly, and try not to lose speed.

Go Up It In Reverse

Sometimes you come across a hill which is so slippery you are ready to give up after no more than a couple of failed attempts and a willing push! Getting your wheels on to virgin snow at the edge may help, depending on the layout of the gutter. A last resort which can have spectacular success particularly in a rear wheel drive car, is to reverse up. It can work at times when there seems to be no danger of success of doing it forwards, and provided it is safe it is worth trying.

OVER-ACCELERATION SKIDS AT FASTER SPEEDS

Just as experienced drivers test dodgy surfaces for braking, they learn to respect slippery surfaces that may, during general driving, induce over-acceleration skids, particularly at corners. In wet weather, by keeping in top gear where possible, they help avoid them (though this is not an excuse for excessive speeds) and they know that in the lower gears on wet, any ferocious acceleration can start wheelspin. On "ice rink" conditions, by contrast, it is possible for feather-light acceleration even in top to provoke wheelspin and the well-informed right toe is therefore a highly disciplined and circumspect fellow in his movements!

Automatic cars can be quite a hazard if you corner near to the limit of adhesion, whether it be too fast on a wet corner or even gingerly on an icy patch. The problem is of an undesired automatic change occurring (up or down) at a critical stage in the corner (for example, if you unintentionally actuate the "kick-down" mechanism) which precipitates a skid.

142

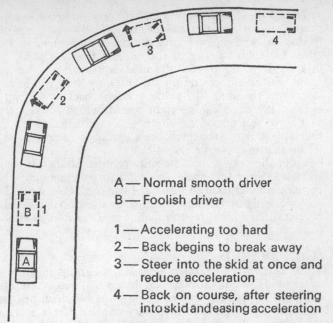

A — Normal smooth driver
B — Foolish driver

1 — Accelerating too hard
2 — Back begins to break away
3 — Steer into the skid at once and reduce acceleration
4 — Back on course, after steering into skid and easing acceleration

Fig. 40. When the back "hangs out" – rear wheel drive.

Readers may have heard the expression "hang the back out". This describes what often happens in a wheelspin skid with rear-wheel drive; the back of the car slides outwards off a corner as in Fig. 40. (Unfortunately sometimes greatly assisted by bad camber, see Fig. 41.) With front-wheel drive the front end may behave similarly though not usually so suddenly or so much.

Fig. 41. Danger of adverse camber.
Bad camber increases the chance of an over-acceleration skid and its severity.

To nip these slides in the bud, as to stop any wheelspin, simply reduce acceleration—*not completely*—sufficient only to stop the wheelspin. To cut it more during a corner could affect the total balance of the car drastically, landing you in a deadly sideslip skid, the next category.

As you ease acceleration to halt wheelspin you have to steer into the skid (the same way the back is sliding) to prevent the car spinning right round, which it has started to do. With front wheel drive you ease acceleration just the same but to straighten the steering is usually enough. (Even that may not be essential.)

From the very second stability returns (sliding or wheelspin dies) steer for where you want to go again and gently increase acceleration to "set" the car back on course. This is done without risking returning to the previous level of acceleration, which was too high, but *is essential to recover from such a skid.*

SIDESLIP SKIDS

I use sideslip as a collective term to group together all other skids not mainly caused by over-fierce acceleration or by harsh braking. The chart on page 145 describes them and shows the likely contributory causes. These skids are terrifying and well-nigh uncontrollable. Correction is so unlikely that prevention is the only real safeguard. Unfortunately they can occur as easily at 60 m.p.h. on wet as at 17 m.p.h. on ice.

Without Warning The Car Ahead Suddenly Spins Off A Straight Road

I have witnessed sheer excess speed causing this several times. A man went 40 m.p.h. on black ice (while others were keeping under 15 m.p.h.); some minor incident caused him to touch the brake or alter steering, and zap! Round he went spinning into the nearest ditch looking very surprised. Another man, charging down a wet motorway, hit some storm water which would have probably been no trouble at a sane speed but which twisted him around in a trice. He was lucky to finish up the grass bank alive. The message is to keep comfortably below borderline top speeds (see page 130) and to hang on to the steering tightly should you come on a surprise collection of water. *At silly speeds a bump, a gust of wind or a bit of aquaplaning, can be the end of you!*

THE DEADLY DANGEROUS SIDESLIP SKID

The whole car appears to slide bodily. A front (or steering) wheel skid can give this impression or **all** wheels, although apparently rolling forward at speed, may **drift**, skidding or sliding off steered course; sometimes called a 4 wheel drift. These skids happen if a car is simply cornered **too fast**, or as a result of hard braking (usually on a corner), or they may be induced if an excessively sharp steering movement is applied, and held, **suddenly.** If steering lock is deliberately and **suddenly** over-applied at any stage during a fast corner the front tyres can slide, even on a dry road. See page 147.

Likely

CONTRIBUTORY CAUSES

(a) MECHANICAL DEFECTS	(b) ROAD CAUSES	(c) HUMAN ERRORS
Treadless tyre(s). Slow puncture. Soft or over-inflated tyre(s). Poor springs or faulty shock absorbers. (These lessen the up and down reaction of the spring after a bump). Front (or back) wheels not having tyres of matched tread pattern, **condition** or, perhaps illegally, type. Overload or unbalanced load.	Wet surface (rain). Slippery surface (oil etc.). Mixed surfaces having different anti-skid properties. Surprise wet patches on generally dry roads. Side-wind. Flood water. Loose surface (wet leaves, gravel, mud etc.). Black ice/"freezing rain". Snow/ice on top of snow. Adverse camber alone **or combined with above.**	Excessive speed for conditions. (Even going straight). Cornering too fast for conditions. Human error in making allowances for (a) and/or (b) is the tragic fault that results in these skids.

145

Cornering Too Fast

Before discussing how to try to avert or reduce disaster once in the grip of a deadly sideslip skid, I will explore the most usual cause. Any moving vehicle tends to drive straight unless effort from the driver steers it. However, with rising speed, *straight on momentum* (weight x speed) and centrifugal force increasingly oppose any steering effort. If speed gets too high relative to the steering applied their combined effect beats the steering grip possible and you go straight on. It follows that slight bends can be taken faster than tight bends. Your safety is wholly dependent on whether your tyres maintain their sideways grip. In the chart on page 145 you can find the other major factors which can precipitate a sideslip skid.

In the sort of sideslip skid which occurs because you really overdo speed into a corner the car skids approximately straight on helplessly, appearing to slide bodily off the far side of the corner because initial steering effort first turns her partly sideways.

So How Can The Fastest Cornering At The Limit Of Safety Be Achieved?

The ability to feel a car's "balance" "through the seat of your pants" and maintain it, perhaps best defines the difference between the skilled driver and the amateur. You can only learn "feel" by trying yourself, cautiously.

Find a deserted straight and dry dual-carriageway with two lanes and adjust to about 40 m.p.h.

From the left lane "throw" the car over to the right lane with a quick steering movement. Almost a twitch on the wheel is enough without altering the position of the hands, instantly straightening and holding rock steady in the new lane.

Notice how much of the car's weight seems to plunge towards the two outside wheels; you can feel those tyres digging into the tarmac. Now "throw" the car back across to the left lane (mirror permitting) and feel the same effect the other way. By this deliberate steering you can set the weight of the car to some extent where you want it.

Theoretically, when cornering, centrifugal force and straight-on momentum try to throw the car out, off the corner. The most important counteracting force is the grip which the two outside tyres manage to hold. The weight is mainly lifted from the inner side of the car so these inner wheels only exert a slight, helpful grip.

The more equally the outer two wheels share the work of opposing centrifugal force and straight-on momentum, the better. If excessive weight lands on the front outer wheel it cannot help but succumb sooner and slide. This is what happens when you brake excessively at a corner.

By cautiously extending experience, you learn just how confidently the weight can be thrown deliberately on to the outside wheels, when a corner is reached, with the tyres still able to accept this onslaught and not lose grip (at the speed and surface conditions prevailing). Begin the technique at lower cornering speeds than you have been used to. Certainly do not start to learn on wet roads, or anything more slippery. It would be easy to throw yourself too hard and into a slide.

You can acquire the knack of angling towards a corner (within the confines of safe road space available) so that when you reach it you can throw the weight gently in the most equal possible way on to the outer wheels to thus achieve the best balance of the car for going round. (Note that at left-hand bends particularly, you dare not risk anything experience hasn't proved O.K. if traffic is, or may be coming.)

I say *gently* throw the weight. You are setting the weight by a deliberate steering movement. At higher speeds or on wet it can happen that too sharp a steering "twitch" makes the front tyres slide immediately. Instead of setting the weight nicely and steering the car round the bend, the front wheels slide and you go straight on. Reduce the steering lock at once to stop this sliding. Should your steering movement instead cause the back of the car to slide out although the front went where you wanted it, you must steer "into" this new rear wheel skid momentarily to regain stability. Either of these dangers is possible if you jerk the steering too hard relative to your speed and the sharpness of the corner. Try not to! This weight-throwing technique needs to be combined with "slow in, fast out" principles, which are explained below, but first . . .

The Limit Of Adhesion

What matters about the limit of adhesion (any conditions) is not where it is or its measurement; *it is the way in which you approach it*. I have discussed keeping a

147

cocoon of safety around your car (page 99). Here it is more than anywhere applicable. Never approach the limit without having room outside your (intended!) line through a bend to recover should you overstep. And, secondly, ensure that any overstepping you do is of a kind from which it is easy to recover. There is a maxim, "slow in, fast out", at corners and here comes part II of fastest safe cornering.

"Slow In, Fast Out"

When you accelerate notice how the front of the car lifts, and the back beds down. You make use of this fact. By steady re-acceleration from half-way round the corner —in practice probably a little earlier—you counteract the natural tendency for most of the weight to bear towards the front outer wheel. Acceleration lifts some of it off the front and transfers it on to the back. You are kept on an even keel going round, "set up for the corner".

Because knowledge of the principles and increasing experience may encourage you to corner faster, I must warn you against being clever at bends, especially blind ones. The old maxim, not to drive faster than would allow you to stop without skidding in the distance you can see to be clear, must rule okay. Traffic may be halted round a bend.

PREVENTING SIDESLIP SKIDS

There is no substitute for slowing sufficiently on approach to a corner to be able to maintain balance going round within the limits of tyre sideways grip.

At normal speeds one eases the accelerator approaching a corner and arrives on "trailing throttle" (foot not completely off the pedal) well inside steering limits, ready for re-accelerating. Faster drivers occasionally approach a corner using brakes.

The Technique Of Braking Into A Corner

Under firm braking the nose of the car dives, bringing more weight on to the front wheels and lifting it off the back ones. This makes cornering at the same time very dangerous because balance is reduced and too much weight is thrown on to the outside front wheel. All heavy braking must therefore be completed on the straight, before beginning to turn.

148

Fig. 42 (a). Leaving maximum safety margin during a fast roundabout.

If you have created your own crisis by slowing down too late your best hope will probably be to brake resolutely to the last inch you dare to keep straight, steering to get you round beginning simultaneously with lifting your foot off the brake. This ensures that the weight gets evenly distributed to the outside wheels; steering throws it outwards; lifting off the brake lets the front rise again and stops too much weight going to the front outside wheel. Slight re-acceleration straight away—even trailing throttle—should, if anything can, hold balance until you steer out of trouble. You have had a fright; avoid them!

This will almost certainly be better than braking so harshly in panic as you come into the corner that you find yourself in a locked brake slide, or a spin, out of control. Normal braking, approaching a corner with good timing, and steadily accelerating out of a corner is excellent practice for establishing confidence.

Allowing Room For Error

If you are of the breed who often find themselves cornering near the limit of adhesion (in youth I was, myself) combine the habit with positioning to allow the maximum space for sliding around. *Think while learning; it is more productive than when you are lying up in Mayday.*

Fig. 42 (a) shows taking a deserted roundabout for straight on, fast, safely, except for some over-acceleration, as will become clear below. We are observing the driver from a safe position well up the road he is heading for. Having slowed enough on entry (from the *top* of the picture), and seeing the in-between road to his *left* clear, he has taken the rest of the roundabout accelerating firmly. Fig. 42 (b) shows the same fast entry line to the roundabout. (Remember, eye-drill established there would be no traffic on the roundabout.)

149

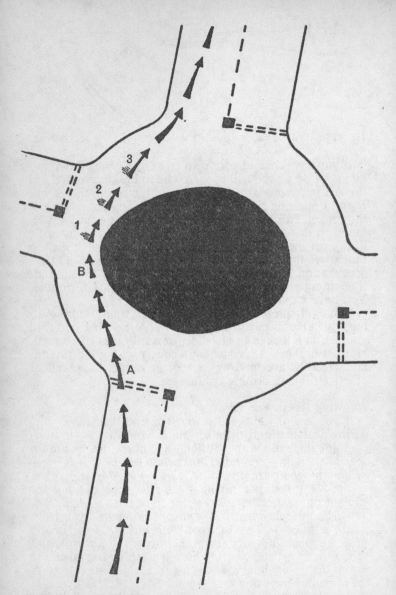

Fig 42. (b). High speed technique for a dry roundabout.

The weight has been thrown gently, well within grip limits, towards the roundabout first as he almost clips the left-hand entry kerb, so maximising safe sliding distance between himself and the roundabout edge, while balance is being established between A and B (Fig. 42 (b)). He expects to travel straight—"balanced"—between A and B. Within a trice of balance going in left, being confirmed and resumption of slight re-acceleration to maintain it, he can and does transfer the weight to where he next wants it by steering right again from B, round the roundabout. From that stage he gets himself tucked in close to the roundabout thereby giving himself all available skidding room to his left where he may now need it. In this lightning roundabout technique you strive to minimise the amount of turning needed at all.

Things can go seriously wrong however. One dare not risk leaving braking as you reach the entry so late that any HARD BRAKING type skid could arise. In Fig. 42 (a) and (b) I have given an artistic impression of what can also happen if over-acceleration during the roundabout causes a skid. In Fig. 42 (b) hatchings on the arrows show how an over-acceleration skid might occur at 1 but instant reduction of acceleration should curtail it by 2, with full control returning around 3. With a closer look at Fig. 42 (a) you can also see the slight over-acceleration skid and that the driver is, in addition, steering into it to correct. The body of the car is dipped evenly towards the outside wheels as you would expect but the steering exhibits "opposite lock" (it is turned the other way to the direction of the car, i.e. into the skid, see page 144) as the rear wheels slip away from the roundabout. With opposite lock, slashed acceleration and luck, control should be regained within a split second. Without these, an element of unplanned reversing may creep in, or worse!

The message of these drawings is that the car is tucked in close, first to the entry kerb, then to the roundabout, always leaving maximum yards to slide on if you misjudge. To induce such skids deliberately is mad but if the tail "hangs out" a couple of feet in error *on a dry road* it is nice to have 24 feet to play with . . .

On wet, even a large safety margin may not prevent you running out of road before corrective action might save you.

Instead of an over-acceleration skid at 1, a front wheel slide might easily have happened, due to too sharp a steering movement being used to transfer the weight at this stage or to too high an entry speed. Instant reduction of steering lock and speed would be vital to kill this slide (page 147). This type of skid is reckoned, depending on degree (and room available), to be marginally safer than an over-acceleration one (especially with rear wheel drive where the back can break away so viciously) but I am not trying to promote either as fun! The most scaring possibility is that both types of skid *can* occur simultaneously—necessitating double lightning-fast corrective action.

When You Haven't Room To Allow Space For Error

Go slower! The Good Lord usually looks after those who take no undue risks.

Eliminating SIDESLIP Even On "Ice-Rink" Roads

Sideslip risk can only be eliminated by slowing down enough in the prevailing conditions so the whole of a bend is negotiable on slight acceleration but with no risk of even a minor over-acceleration wheelspin. Should one still happen, counteract it by reducing acceleration instantly, just sufficiently to stop it (see page 144).

Sweeping Wide Bends

A long wide bend need not always be driven as the normal and acceptable continuous curve. On the comparative safety of dry road faster drivers may prefer to test the following technique. It obviates the problem which can exist ordinarily of the feeling of grip (or lack of it) losing definition. Having learned the technique it need not be applied as routine, or even as everyday practice; suffice that the ability to feel balance thus ingrained will be instinctively available on that ubiquitous "one day" when panic could kill.

Nearly all the road width is required so it is not for slower drivers owing to the nuisance to faster traffic wishing to overtake. Even for the fast driver it assumes his mirror art is fully developed! The need for space limits full safe use of the technique to dual carriageways although the principle may be partially applied on very wide two-way bends provided you keep within the limits of your own side, well out of the way of any approaching traffic *and vision through the whole bend is unrestricted.*

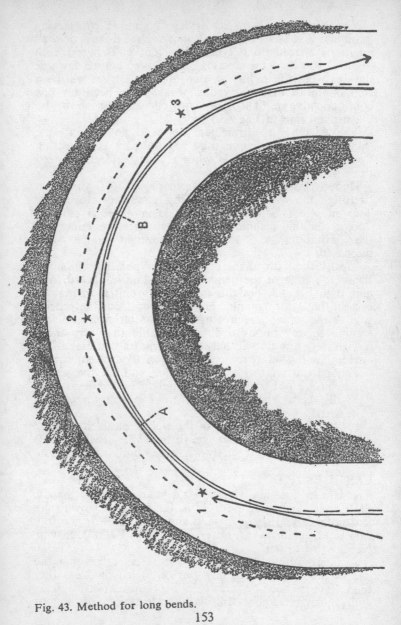

Fig. 43. Method for long bends.

153

You assess the bend as having a number of steering "points". Fig. 43 1, 2 and 3 shows how these "points" might be spaced on a typical long curve. Between each "point" you hold the steering on a curved course towards the next, but the radius of each of these curves will be a fraction more than the radius would have been for one continuous curve. (The continuous curve is also shown by the broken line in Fig. 43.)

The effect is to straighten the bend apart from the "points". A short curve may require only one steering "point" to "straighten" it while a long bend could need three or even four "points".

Under "fastest cornering", from page 146, I discussed "setting" the weight of the car by a steering movement. This in effect is what you are doing at each steering "point" in this technique; you must therefore remember the limitations to "setting" the weight which were discussed.

Ideally the path of the car between "points" will shave the inside edge of the bend or of the line as shown at A and B in Fig. 43, but this is less important than making certain that your "points" are well away from the outside edge while under no circumstances getting yourself close enough to any opposite direction traffic to worry them. Your safety margin will only be as large as you make it.

Here are the safety reasons for this method of cornering:
a) Apart from the "points" where you set the weight you are not cornering so acutely. The car is marginally better balanced therefore for any unexpected emergency.
b) The deliberate setting of the weight on each "point" gives you more exact feel of how she is balanced. It confirms you are safely within the limits of adhesion.

LAST RESORTS

Too late to question why, you got yourself into a ghastly SIDESLIP. Suddenly the front is dancing to her own tune and nothing you try is making any difference, or she (the car) is going sideways, or even backwards. Keep your wits. Never yield to panic.

A quick action may save you but remember that the decent thing may be to bow out through a hedge rather than have a head-on crash, killing innocent as well as guilty. Circumstances will flash such points of honour

154

through your hopefully decisive (at the time!) brain helping you judge the proper course of action.

You'll be thankful for the instinct of self-preservation coupled with acquired understanding of the importance of balance especially if you *have* allowed room for mistakes.

Catching A SIDESLIP In Its Early Stages

Steering to straighten the front wheels into line or nearer into line with the back ones, and getting them to roll again if they are locked, are the priorities. (Turning the steering beyond straight—i.e. to "opposite lock"—could make matters worse unless the rear wheels are already skidding sideways.) See pages 135 and 151.

Now straight, but probably going in a dangerous direction, braking may be next essential before steering to try to clear a crash. Alternatively, within a trice of even a vague feeling of grip returning, you may be forced to try and steer to miss something. This will again tend to throw the weight on to only two wheels but skill and luck could take you out of trouble.

The greatest quality in driving is having nerves of steel; the supreme folly is to take advantage of having them. They may help you, however, though you might need to have some rallying experience tucked under your belt as well, should you find yourself, for example, in circumstances where you have got into a sideslip which has almost run its course. Sometimes you can recognise through experience that the way not to finish up biffing a tree or whatever is to accelerate and "hang the back out", simultaneously steering into the newly created over-acceleration skid. A precision-tuned rally car would probably be a prerequisite for success, to save your neck!

A corner or a road surface can take you unawares. Imagine unexpected black ice getting you into a sideslip skid at 35 m.p.h., mild initially but threatening to get worse on a long corner with bad camber aggravating the trouble. Holding the accelerator dead on the exact road speed (neither accelerating nor allowing engine braking) can sometimes precariously maintain balance until you reach the straight and have a chance to slow gradually and in safety. Rather like walking on a tightrope, one slip and you fall off the road. The hope would be that the slide off the corner would subside before the wheels touched the edge or you hit an oncoming vehicle. Drop acceleration just a fraction too much and the slide takes charge; accelerate a razor's edge more than it needs and you get an over-acceleration skid, in which the car may spin before you can steer into it.

Too Late! A SIDESLIP Has Turned You Almost, Or Completely Round, Or The Car Is Spinning Further Round Than Just Backwards

Don't "freeze" in terror. Most spins subside within 180° and the car rolls on backwards. Getting the steering straight helps this happen. Quick wits in putting the brakes on once she is running back may save you from smashing something solid unnecessarily.

Having come to rest, move the car out of danger if possible, or abandon ship and comfort passengers. Don't sit and be hit!

Let Skidding Fools Miss You

Suppose you see a fastard careering towards you out of a bend so fast, he is likely to skid into your road space. It is here that the Buppies (see page 13) are sorted out from the very advanced. The former sail on to probable disaster, hypnotised as is a rabbit by a weasel, by the super-speed of the approaching car.

The experienced have estimated where the fool will skid and in the half or quarter second of thinking time for keeping alive, have either slowed, so the chap will skid in front, or speeded up, so he will skid behind, or more likely, slowed and got as far away from the maniac as possible to avoid the hurtling mass of death as it skids past.

As you see him sliding helplessly at you, you may if there is no avoiding it be best to angle your car so that he only hits your tail end, or, so that your two cars will only "bounce" softly off one another, by making sure you hit parallel, whole side length to whole side length.

UNDERSTEER AND OVERSTEER

Most cars are designed to understeer. In normal (non-skidding) cornering the car runs, instead of on the precise arc the steering would theoretically determine, slightly wider—a fraction outside the curve steered. All the wheels "slip" by a tiny amount—invisible to the naked eye—further out than the curve to which they are pointing and thus the circle radius which the vehicle as a whole follows is fractionally greater than the precise circle steered.

In designing a car to understeer the makers ensure that the amount by which the front tyres "slip" is always slightly more than the back tyres. Thus at ultimate cornering adhesion speeds the front tyres should slide first— the increasing "slip" as the limit of cornering grip is reached comes to the "breakaway" point earlier at the front.

If a car oversteers on the other hand the rear wheels will tend to break away first, the breakaway itself being so swift and complete few drivers can cope. For these and more technical reasons it has become accepted that an understeering car is safest.

The difference (or lack of it) between front and rear tyre pressures as recommended by car manufacturers may be as much as 20 pounds per square inch and is scientifically calculated to ensure slight understeer. Keep to the recommendations or you may find yourself with dangerous oversteer. Incorrect pressures are illegal.

11

VERY FAST DRIVING

THE OVERALL SPEED LIMIT

For the disciplined driver speeds above 100 m.p.h. at times, even on our crowded roads, are safer than 40 m.p.h. for a "my speed" Buppy (see page 14).

To all appearances the 70 m.p.h. limit was brought in to show that the Government was "doing something" about accidents. Introducing it at the same time as the breathalyser defied sense, making it impossible to distinguish results from either measure. I have seen no statistics showing conclusively that the 70 m.p.h. limit has reduced accidents.

Indeed the 70 m.p.h. speed limit has probably *increased* accidents. Most drivers have a natural limit at which their wits are sharp. For a substantial proportion this is well over 70 m.p.h.; force them back even a few m.p.h. and they become bored and drive "wide asleep". Such fatigue, especially on long journeys, has major accident potential. Concentration cluttered by looking out for police also portends danger. Having the limit encourages close-up bunching in outside lanes. Apart from idiotic 70 m.p.h.—"at the limit"—obstructors, more reasonable drivers also occupy the outside lane too long. Instead of accelerating quickly past a group of lane 2 vehicles going nearly as fast as themselves, thus getting back to lane 2/1 and well segregated quickly, drivers hang next to each other for miles as they inch past—barred from better driving by the limit. As a result high speed packs of cars form—to hurtle on as if in formation—instead of separating themselves out as common sense, safety (and much of this book!) urge. Think how often a brief burst of acceleration would enable a "speed limit appointed" pack leader to regain lane 2 at once, and thus free the rest of the pack to disperse straightaway.

I would throw out the overall speed limit. Far better to catch the few maniacs who endanger life in heavily populated 30 m.p.h. limits than to gong safe drivers at 70 m.p.h. plus.

I cannot in a book about safety leave out very fast driving just because of a silly British law. In some other countries there are no overall limits. Although I would not set *any* limit (a limit can encourage a false feeling of safety up to it), for myself I feel that on motorways and very good roads 90/100 m.p.h. (on dry only) is as fast as my eyes and brain can cope should the unpredictable suddenly arise. To exceed 70/80 m.p.h. *at night*—no matter how fabulous car or lights is lunacy. "Night eyes" cannot spear the darkness safely much over 80 m.p.h.

SELF DISCIPLINE

The chief qualifications for very fast driving are self discipline, wisdom and many years' experience. Until 200,000 miles +, one is a babe in road-craft and know-how. Many "young bloods" die because they refuse to concede this. 17–24 are the "insurance proven" dangerous years; the years when most, on account of their age, cannot have had the learning miles. Self discipline must include accepting how slow your reactions are, and if they, or concentration, are being affected by illness, tiredness or anger. It demands adjustment of fastest speeds downwards to compensate. Few like to admit failings, which makes this discipline a test of character. At 35 your reactions *are* slower than at 20 years old.

By very fast driving I do not only mean high speed driving. I refer to the ability to maintain high average speeds. On winding or busy roads very fast driving could be under 45 m.p.h. all the time. Keeping the highest speed compatible with safety, and ever changing to match conditions, is the secret of the very fast driver who never scares others or himself.

"DESIGNED-IN" SAFETY

Family cars in good order can be driven briskly quite safely; high performance versions may not be safe any faster, contrary to their superior image; while their engines may be hotted-up, weight distribution, suspension, brakes etc. may *not* be, and allowances must be made. VERY FAST driving at its pinnacle demands the designed in safety of a car purpose-built for speed. Among the few thoroughbred makes that qualify rank names like AC, Aston Martin, Ferrari, Lamborghini and Lotus.

Four-Wheel-Drive

Decades after the demise of the British invented Ferguson FF, continued pioneering, pre-eminently by Audi, has brought four-wheel-drive to mass production. Their four-wheel-drive, enhanced by their computerised anti-lock braking system (ABS), provides a degree of primary safety akin to that of the exotic machinery above. After several years' ownership of an Audi Avant Quattro, I can vouch for their inclusion among the elite.

The Quattro features continuous four-wheel-drive. On dry, you drive confident that cornering adhesion will exceed all normal expectations. On wet, the grip on bends is uncanny, all but matching the *dry-road* performance of two-wheel-drive. Traction/grip are so evenly distributed my tyre-life has soared 50% despite pushing this sure-footed pedigree consistently to its limits.

Over limits yes, the Quattro will slide but she is forgiving; side-slip type skids are not only less vicious, the responses to corrective action are ultra-quick by comparison with a typical two-wheel-drive. Over-acceleration type skidding is negligible on dry and difficult to achieve on wet, again, due to the spread of power to the four wheels. However, one drawback that must be noted is that aqua-planing is undiminished by four-wheel-drive. Whereas with front-wheel-drive wheelspin may alert you (see page 130), with four-wheel-drive you can be put in peril by excessive speed without warning, just as with rear-wheel-drive.

The four-wheel-drive snow/mud traction is spectacular. And the two differentials can be temporarily locked, improving it still further. Imagine starting off on packed-down snow up a 1 in 7 gradient in reverse, without wheelspin! In deeply rutted snow, where others slip, slide and stick, imprisoned by the ruts, the Quattro—as long as there is sufficient ground clearance—effortlessly makes new tracks. Being able to stop and start at will on the worst possible surfaces gives the Quattro driver a huge advantage. He can choose his moment and pick his way past others getting stuck; he can wait bemused while lesser cars take a run at a tricky patch. However, despite the marvellous traction, he must not be fooled about *stopping*. He must never forget that, although four-wheel-drive allows slightly superior engine braking, the footbrake may be as powerless on ice as any other! At the low speeds appropriate to deep, loose snow, locked wheels, despite the loss of steering control resulting, may slow the car quicker than anti-lock braking can manage. This is because snow piles up in front of each wheel in a snow plough effect. Specifically for these very slow conditions the Audi ABS can be switched off. How good it is in all other circumstances I turn to next.

Anti-Lock Braking System

The computer-controlled anti-lock braking system on the Audi transforms emergency braking. No matter how harsh the braking no wheel can lock, even on wet. Working on each wheel individually, the ABS reduces the brake pressure to any wheel that is about to lock by just enough to stop it sliding. The ideal fastest stop described on page 134 is achieved regardless of driver skill. As if that were not a supreme enough advance there is a life-saving bonus. Steering control cannot be lost, because the front wheels cannot slide. You can steer normally under fiercest braking. So novel is this phenomenon, related to basic driver training hitherto (i.e. keep steering as straight as possible), that you need to do some testing to "re-learn" your emergency drill to prepare yourself for the time that a swerve stop may save a formerly unavoidable accident.

Having spelt out the advantages of four-wheel-drive and ABS, I must endorse Audi's own literature by sounding a note of caution. Never let this primary safety of the Quattro seduce you into risk-taking through excess speed.

Mechanical Condition

Tremendous stresses are created by fast driving. The thoroughbred, no less than the ordinary car, must be maintained mechanically 100% to perform safely, for your own and the public's safety. It is up to you.

Features of a Thoroughbred Fast Car

Having been also the owner of two Lotus cars I hope the reader will excuse a Lotus flavour here! Features which set the thoroughbred apart include the safety resulting from reserves of instant power (squirtability for overtaking and precision flexibility for "setting" balance during fast corners), fingertip steering even at 120 m.p.h., vice-like braking even from ultra-high speed. Any who have had to emergency brake a family car from top speed will know the sickening feeling of uncontrollability which can result. The Lotus driver survives without such hair-raising prospects.

Most spectacular among his car's attributes is the superglue predictability of the grip going round bends. The Lotus can safely whirl round curves at 70 m.p.h. which would find some saloons squealing at 40 m.p.h. Another impressive feature is the suspension, which lets the Lotus wheels ripple across all the bumps with almost total elimination of up and down pitching by the bodywork. (The latter, especially on corners, undermines tyre grip.)

Lotus acceleration is breathtaking. Oft-repeated experiences scarcely dilute the thrill of it. 0–100 m.p.h. in a single burst (on dry road, of course) will put butterflies in the strongest stomach.

THE DRAWBACKS OF SPEED

So extreme is the difference in "drive-ability" between hand-built cars such as the Lotus and everyday models it is hard to appreciate their astonishing potential until you have sampled such performance. The way in which mobile bottlenecks of traffic to be overtaken (doing their best at ordinary speeds), can be viewed as subtle points of interest instead of major headaches, is amazing.

Fast driving in such cars requires assuming everybody you pass has no idea you are there. Even the conscientious mirror user may not appreciate how suddenly he can be caught up. Overtaking possibilities appear in a different perspective to the Lotus driver.

Even though they may have noted your arrival behind, the moment you select to pass is often a huge surprise to other motorists. (The most likely drivers to spot your arrival behind are other fast drivers in above average machines. Similar experience has raised their reaction speeds, anticipation and motoring sensitivity to a high degree of excellence.)

A major Lotus advantage is the ease with which, after cutting speed to pass at a safe differential, the original cruising speed can be resumed in a trice. A family car might need half a mile to build up to a similar cruising speed and its driver may be loathe to cut any of it in consequence. He is tempted to make chancy passes, which is deadly. Not so the Lotus man; he can slow right down knowing that once he sees all is clear he can bolt past into a safe gap. No fear for him of a "nasty bit of work" who will "race" and try to stop him getting past—because by the time the horrible driver (there are a few) has decided to accelerate, it is too late. *The Lotus has gone*.

One drawback, for it is not always allowed for by others, is the capability of the Lotus to corner as if on rails, faster than approaching traffic about to come into view conceivably expects. Therefore although you may delight in cornering at speeds verging on the incredible, because you could scare someone into panic—you must not. It is different when you can see through the corner.

On blind bends, only madmen risk running into stopped traffic, a crash or an overtaking vehicle approaching round the corner. Even when cornering at speeds wisely related to vision, fast drivers usually cover the brake during the critical seconds when any danger could be revealed. They always aim to position to allow for straight line braking should any emergency arise in the unfolding scene.

Slight cutting of speed during a dangerous stage by braking may improve the technique, because on seeing any emergency the car is already partly in braking equilibrium.

Becoming airborne over hump-backs can happen in fast driving, though one should not go so fast; don't brake—you would land on locked wheels; and don't turn the steering—which could have the same effect.

ILLUSIONS OF SECURITY IN HAIRY MACHINES

There is a limit even for a Lotus. Fix that firmly in your mind; especially for your first 100,000 "Lotus" miles, keep on remembering it. No matter how good the machine is, it is driven by an imperfect person, you. Only you can make the proper allowance for your weaknesses, perhaps night eyesight or slower-than-average reactions.

To become a master driver, master yourself. Self-control and self-knowledge are the rules for very advanced driving.

In your early ownership of a fast car be content to drive it far below its capacity. These are learning days; in safe conditions, experiment with just how the car can accelerate, steer and brake. Get acquainted with when it will skid. Learn the car's reactions in dry, and later damp or icy conditions on clear roads so that your mind will be attuned to the limitations. For the first 25,000 miles drive little faster than you would a family car. Learn carefully over many months so that you come to know what you can do.

One danger is to imagine—particularly on wet—that speed is lower than it is. I find Lotus speeds invariably higher on the same wet corners where I drive several miles per hour slower in an ordinary car.

A study of the skidding chapter shows the need for keeping the right balance of initial speed, steering and acceleration during cornering. Cornering near the limit of adhesion at the higher speeds possible in fast cars requires greater sensitivity to judge balance, and an error—not appreciating how near the limit you are—may therefore be more dangerous.

Reasons are these:

a) Recovery action if tyre grip breaks away is harder in proportion to higher speed (although to be fair the car may prove to be more forgiving, it's hardly a clever policy to try it!).

b) In an ordinary saloon car even heavy-footed acceleration as you leave a corner may not cause an over-acceleration skid whereas a touch on the throttle at the same place and speed could in the Lotus. With surging power under your toe you dare not waggle it carelessly.

A GLIMPSE AT THE FAST DRIVING EXPERT

Because of his car's direct steering action most bends don't require the driver to alter his hand position from "10 to 2". The wheel turns, the arms bend but the hands remain. He

163

can have no doubt (the amount off-centre of his arms tells him subconsciously) how much steering lock he has applied at any moment. This is very useful in getting the feel of what is happening to the steering wheels.

When cornering at speed he may push with his left foot against the floor beside the pedals if there is room to help lock himself into the driving seat and stop his bottom sliding.

To a passenger he appears almost constantly to alternate between light or firm braking—never more nor less than required—and resumption of swift acceleration. Even on motorways he rarely holds one speed long. There is constant action or reaction; the slightest doubt ahead is met with instant speed reduction. The thought that it may be nothing serious is rejected along with wait-and-see thoughts, for without immediate braking control being gathered he knows it could be too late. Very advanced drivers try to be ready *before* emergencies.

His observation seems miraculous and the religious way he slows for hazards more than almost anyone else—despite going faster than they would dream of when it is safe—appears out of keeping with such fast general driving. At the unbelievable speeds available to him on the unrestricted motorways found in some countries you will note that he will treat a mere speck on the horizon as a major alert for openers; only once able to identify what it is will he resume his earlier pace if safe.

At any high speed one notices his concentration is on "shall I have to brake" and when he does he always begins unexpectedly early. He understands braking distances at top speed are far greater than any eye could judge within feet. The good fast driver keeps an immense safety margin in hand.

His speed is usually only very high when the road is empty. He then uses the middle of it frequently, to give extra manœuvreability should a tyre burst, etc.

On clear, see-through curves, he takes maximum advantage of any camber and may "cut" or "straighten" these corners when no-one else is around. But he would never "cut" a corner if it meant putting the car on the wrong side of the road inches from a blind gateway or lane. There's too much danger of someone nosing out, or swinging out of it, not expecting him to be coming on the "wrong" side.

Overbrow Following

This principle applies to long bends as well as where vision is limited by the contours. The very advanced driver will take a blind brow, or a long curve where he cannot see right round the corner, faster when he is following somebody than he would if he were out in front! Here is why:

He knows that if there is congestion or even a pile-up over the brow, or perhaps an accident half-way round the bend, it is down to him to pull up in time. As the chap in front reaches the brow or gets into the main part of the corner the advanced driver makes sure he is positioned so that the gap between them is respectable relative to the speed; he thus ensures his stopping power; at the same time, if it is possible without sacrificing this safe gap at any stage, he keeps the rear lamp cluster of that car ahead within sight as it glides over the brow or carries on—always on the point of disappearing—round the corner. By this subtle use of the fellow ahead as his "eyes" he finds he can afford to go a little faster than had he been leader of the pack arriving "blind" over the brow or pioneering through the bend. At night you may be able to watch several cars ahead on a bend, for example where rear lights shine through railings which obscure by day. On dual-carriageways you may see two or three safely over a brow at once but keep their brake lights in view! The rooftop alone is *not* enough to show if someone is stopping.

12

CRASHES AND
EXTRAORDINARY CIRCUMSTANCES

From the torrent of statistics available one could devote a lifetime to researching accident causes. However, among the killer crashes that should be avoided at practically any cost to safeguard life I would list the worst as these:

1. Being hit by a train on a level crossing.
2. Knocking cyclists or motorcyclists flying.
3. Hitting pedestrians.
4. Hitting or being hit side-on (the doors of a car are usually the weakest point).
5. Head-on into another moving vehicle.

6. Head-on into solid objects such as trees, parked vehicles, brick walls, etc.
7. Skids resulting in hitting lamp posts, etc., which can cut sideways through passenger or driver's compartment.

Individual differences of speed, confines of space, etc., might place these in a different order, but the list probably covers the most fatal types of accident.

SAFETY BELTS

The purpose of belts is to stop you being thrown against anything hard, or even out of the car, in an emergency or crash. Vulnerable parts like the skull get mashed on metal and glass time after time, even when the smash is foreseen. The philosophical arguments about individual freedom under the law ignore this. Although a belt itself occasionally may cause injury I feel the present law is right. Rear passengers still arrive unannounced in the front head first (where it kills) so often, I myself hope rear belt law comes soon. The law already encourages you to carry young children in the back and in a proper child safety seat/harness. Belt carrycots in a purpose-made harness. Fasten all these firmly (likewise early non-inertia adult belts). The Code also reminds you about child safety locks.

POINTS TO REMEMBER IF YOU HAVE AN ACCIDENT

You must stop. If you find no damage or injury has been caused to another person, vehicle, animal or property outside your vehicle, then, with the abominable modern tendency for people to make untrue and preposterous allegations of blame, you may be well advised to go quietly on your way before being accused of dangerous this or careless that. Failure to stop is a very serious criminal offence and the penalties are therefore accordingly fierce. You may not assume that there is no damage or injury; you must stop and make sure.

Where there has clearly been damage or injury as above then, as well as stopping, you must at the time give your own name and address and the vehicle owner's as well if it is different, plus the vehicle's registration number to anyone having reasonable grounds for requiring them. If anyone has been injured you also need to produce your Certificate of Insurance for them to take details. Since an injured party or anyone on their behalf could hardly be regarded as unreasonably asking to see your Certificate of Insurance in circumstances of an injury accident the wise thing is to carry the Certificate in the car. It is also wise to carry your M.O.T. Certificate if you have one because should the police arrive on the scene they would be entitled to ask to see it.

As long as you have been able to comply with the above details the law demands no more of you. Only if you do not give the details required to any person having reasonable grounds for needing them or you cannot show them your insurance certificate do you have to report the accident to the police. Then you have to do this as soon as practicable and anyway within 24 hours, remembering that they may ask to see your Certificate of Insurance and also any M.O.T. Certificate if applicable.

Do not forget to obtain all the information you are entitled to—in particular you want to have sight of the other party's insurance certificate—and note it all down. Witnesses often almost fall over themselves in their rush to leave the scene uninvolved, but do try and persuade them to give you their names and addresses and perhaps a statement of what they saw. Remember, as a witnessing driver hastens off, you might be lucky and trace him through the Licensing Authority by his number. If any office or house windows overlook the scene, enquiry might find someone who saw the accident. Usually one or two people, probably fellow motorists, will offer evidence. If you are innocent, a good witness (unless in a fatal accident) will rarely be called to Court. A guilty party hardly ever goes to Court if you have a couple of witnesses, and you can explain this to them.

The essential need for the witness is to save your driving reputation. His existence helps prevent the other driver spinning some fairy-tale later, as is all too common.

No matter whose fault you may believe it to be at the time, *you must remember to inform your insurance company*. Otherwise you can find yourself unprotected in court facing ruination if judgement is (rightly or wrongly) held against you. They will advise you on claiming against the other driver if appropriate.

Unfortunately a "no claim" bonus is not a "no blame" bonus and in cases where you are innocent you may need to pin down with your insurance company how your no claims discount can be protected from the outset. All measurements, photographs or other factual evidence you can gather will probably help in the event of any legal entanglement and it is wise to sketch the scene while it is clear in your mind. Measure distances from the edge of the road, skid marks, etc., if it is possible to do so safely, and record them on the drawings you make.

You must not admit blame even if you are at fault. To say nothing on the subject may be a condition of your insurance policy.

Even if you believe a crash was not your fault, if people are injured, you naturally have a human duty to see that the best is done for them before any consideration of the points raised above. See page 126 for advice.

RUNAWAY CAR (BRAKE FAILURE)

Continually "pump" the brake pedal; there is always a chance you may regain some braking. The handbrake may be more help than you can tell. Also, "smash" gears down —straight to 2nd, then first. Hoot and flash lights—both in quick succession, to warn. If you are not on a hill, these actions may suffice. In general, miss anything, rather than hit something solid. On a downhill, however, you may need to choose the lesser evil of bumping kerbs, grazing walls, etc., holding the steering wheel tight as you do, early, rather than later, when you have built up momentum and the potential damage has passed out of control.

BURST TYRES AND PUNCTURES

With a puncture—which can lead to a burst—you get warnings, the steering feels odd and wandery, you get a bumpier ride and there is loss of normal "balance". Always check if you think something is wrong rather than drive on. A weekly pressure check should alert you to any slow puncture needing attention.

A burst (blow out) is rare. If it happens, you may suddenly hear the bumping noises as the tyre carcass rolls across the wheel rim from one side to the other, or (if you have hit something sharp lying in the road) you may anticipate the burst; however sometimes your only warning is sudden reduced control, with the car trying to veer to one side.

Bursts are not funny, but in the absence of panic, should not be any reason for causing an accident. The important thing is to hold on to the steering confidently and to use strength, if required, to steer past danger. With luck the traffic situation will allow you to steer gently into the side as, with your foot off the accelerator, your speed slows *of its own accord* to a stop. The one thing not to do is jam on the brakes! If at all possible do not touch the brake, just let your momentum peter out. If you do have to brake be ever so gentle on the pedal and be ready to grip the steering as you do it.

Most bursts, if they don't result from running with the tyre soft (see page 126), are probably originally caused by hitting kerbs some hundreds of miles earlier—see page 179. The advanced driver, especially the fast advanced driver, examines his tyres for visible damage, particularly bulging of the walls, at least once a week. He gets down to look at the inside as well as the outside wall of each tyre.

ACCELERATOR STICKS FULL ON
Action: de-clutch (or move automatic lever to "N") at once. Switch off engine quickly, before the engine "revs" its head off. At the same time pull safely over to the edge of the road. Take care not to switch the ignition key all the way to a steering lock position or you may be in even more trouble! Add hazard lights if necessary until you sort things out.

RUNNING OUT OF PETROL OR BLOCKAGE
The danger is that the engine splutters and fails just as you are on maximum acceleration passing someone. While a blockage may be an act of God, the advanced driver can develop a habit which should avoid foolhardy running out. The required habit is to associate switching on the ignition with checking the petrol guage. A decision can thus be made before you move off whether more petrol will be needed to complete the journey being made. If it will, you can straightaway concentrate on remembering to pull in at the next petrol station and eliminate the running out risk. To the advanced driver, running with a nearly full tank seems no more difficult than running with a nearly empty tank; he therefore does so with the added advantages that muck in the bottom of the tank does not get sucked through to the engine and, in winter, condensation (and therefore water) is less likely to form in the air space above the petrol within the tank—either of which can lead to engine misfiring or failure.

ENGINE STALLS (STOPS)

Action: Hazard lights straight on. As a life-saver, if about to be hit (e.g. on a level crossing) *move on the starter* in first gear (not possible with automatic transmission). The battery should take you to nearby safety. If it does not and a train is going to hit you don't just sit there! (People do.)

BREAKDOWNS ON FAST ROADS

Again, if you break down on a busy main road, don't wait to be hit. Try and push the car or "drive" it on the starter as above, on to the verge if there is one, or the hard shoulder. Have someone alert traffic if possible and also put out a red accident triangle 50–150 metres back. Open the boot lid and lean the spare wheel, or back seat, etc., against the rear bumper. This is a universally-recognised breakdown signal. Above all get the vehicle on to a safe place.

13

BRIEF NOTES ON EUROPEAN DRIVING

Most of the following applies throughout the continent although minor differences exist in the various countries; the signs shown are French, being the most likely country for people to start driving on the right. Most bookshops and motoring organisations can easily supply up-to-date additional information on individual countries.

HEADLAMPS

Your lamps must dip *right*. Mask a small triangle or other shape of headlamp glass with black tape as instructed by your car book of words or the manufacturer's agent. Or use clip-on yellow covers if available, which bend the light through the yellow lenses.

INSURANCE

Make sure your policy is right or you may be forced to buy a more expensive one at Customs, or return home. Although some policies automatically offer minimum legal European cover this may only equate to a third party basis; rather than discover that, too late, a Green Card should make sure you are covered to the extent customary in Britain.

1

4

2

3

5

6

7

Fig. 44. Some continental signs.
All these signs have red borders, except 7, which has a white background, no border, and a shaded horn crossed out by a blue line.
The key numbers are referred to in the text.

NO PANIC ABOUT DRIVING ON THE RIGHT

Even on your first trip it is easier than you might think.
The influence of other traffic helps keep you "right" but
you need to be more alert on empty roads. A passenger
who occasionally shouts "keep right" helps in the first

hours, especially at night. Plan to arrive in daylight. Especially if you are alone, repeat to yourself for the first few hours "keep right" and have a post card with these words facing you on the dashboard. Be extra careful on entering or leaving roundabouts where one is apt to go wrong. You turn right into roundabouts.

The most likely time for forgetting this keeping right is when trying to find your way, or if you are on a long clear road and suddenly meet somebody coming towards you. In the latter instance instinct is apt to take you left. So you must prepare your mind by repeating "keep right". The risk of forgetting diminishes after a few hundred miles until you get home—then you have to tell yourself to "keep left" but that is easier!

No one wants to be confused with hundreds of detailed notes just before setting out on holiday (or business) and I think all you need worry about are the few signs and principles which differ from British practice.

DIFFERENT PRINCIPLES
Parking
Continentals rarely stop on the roadside like we do. Outside towns there is almost no parking except off the road on the verge out of danger. How sensible! In towns and villages pavement parking seems the general rule or in clearly signed wide roads.

Priorité A Droite
The logical simplicity of this rule is great. Unless sign-posted otherwise you give way at any sort of junction to anybody who is coming from a road to your right. It is on the minor road networks particularly that you need to keep your wits about you with regard to this rule. Note that anyone approaching on a road to your left has to give way to you; thus your prime concern, without dismissing the left entirely, will be to focus attention on the road(s) to your right, giving way as required. The Continentals make great use of this law. The first time some-one shoots in front of you from the right can be frightening, but you get used to it!

On the trunk and main city routes this principle is overruled as and where sign-posted. Out in the country sign No. 1, Fig. 44, appears before each junction as you come up to it, to remind you that your main road is given priority. In villages or towns sign 2, Fig. 44, is frequent and has the same meaning. As a confirming reminder, if in doubt, you can often see the give-way or stop sign facing the incoming road at the intersection before you reach it, or a thick stop line painted against them.

By these signs the important roads retain priority most of the time but you must impress on your mind that if you suddenly come upon an area where such signs are omitted, or if you leave the main route, then priority reverts to the right and it's your job to watch it!

Where two trunk roads cross, sign 3, Fig. 44, strategically placed to warn you in time, is one you must remember because, as the roads are of equal importance, priority to the right applies.

Equally, on the minor roads you are well sign-posted to give way at main roads and to allow priority to the right at all others. (Similar give-way and stop signs to ours and sign 4, Fig. 44, or at more dangerous junctions, sign 5.)

On roundabouts don't forget to give way to the right in addition to circulating the "wrong" way, i.e. to the right. (You give way to people joining, which is the opposite rule to ours.)

Policemen

Pass in front or behind them as appropriate. They seem less tied to the rule book than their British counterparts, although they may carry guns!

Hooting

Over much of the continent *no hooting* is allowed in the towns. Sign 6, Fig. 44, will be noticed somewhere on the outskirts to tell you and sign 7 ends the prohibition as you leave the city.

Honk! Honk!

Just as our lorry drivers flash headlights to tell anyone overtaking them they are clear to move in, in Europe the technique is a loud blast or two on the horn. This is a little shattering if you don't know to expect it.

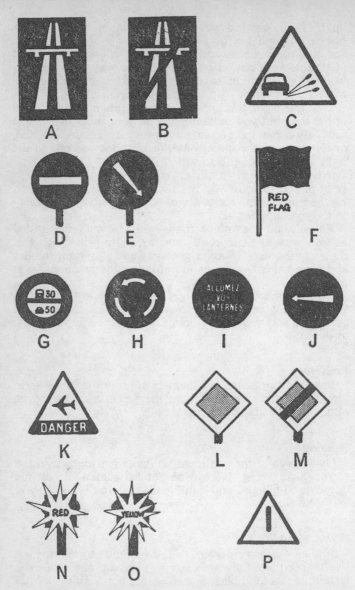

Fig. 45. More European signs.
Key to this figure is on page 176

174

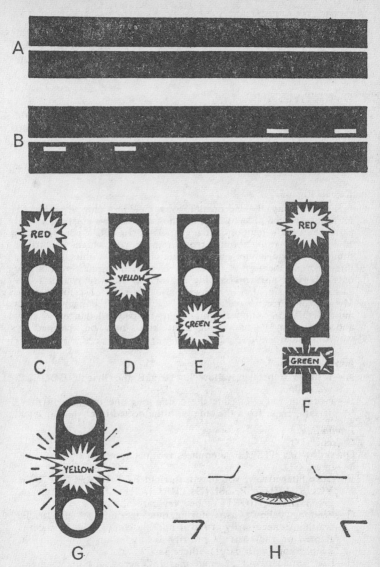

Fig. 46. Continental traffic lights, "bollards", "double" lines.
Key to this figure is on page 176

DIFFERENT SIGNS

Most continental signs are placed on the right hand edge; they are rarely duplicated on the left as in Britain. Figs. 44, 45 and 46 show the important ones which differ from their British equivalents.

OVERTAKING

To help you, *be sure to have a well adjusted left wing mirror*. It assumes life-saving importance in right hand driving.

Key to Fig. 45.

A—motorway, B—end of motorway, C—loose chippings, D and E (blue)—placed side by side 'as shown mark the start of a dual carriageway, F—temporary danger, G—lorries 30 k.p.h. and cars 50 k.p.h., H—roundabout; arrows remind you which way to go round, I—white letters on deep blue circle show obligatory rule; this example means put lights on, J—turn in direction of arrow only, K—you are approaching an aircraft runway; watch for a flashing alert signal, L—yellow box means start of priority road, M—end of priority road, N—red flashing light; danger and you must STOP, O—yellow flashing light; unspecified danger so slow and take care, P—hazard of some kind; may be specified by wording underneath.

Key to Fig. 46.

A—a single unbroken yellow line equals the British DOUBLE white line.

B—a broken line alongside the continuous one means you may, if safe, cross from the side with the dotted line while it lasts.

Traffic lights
C—red, STOP.
D—yellow BY ITSELF announces red just coming.
E—green, GO.
F—green filter arrow; you may turn right BUT TRAFFIC FROM YOUR LEFT, PASSING THROUGH THE LIGHTS *on green* HAS PRIORITY; be very careful.
G—*Flashing* yellow: used during quiet periods to save traffic waiting unnecessarily at red if nothing comes. The junction is treated on the basis:— priority to anyone on your right but keep going (with care!) otherwise.
H—Flat circle about 3″ high and 18″ across, lit up at night. Treat like a mini ("magic") roundabout. You keep right of it just as you keep left of the British ones.

176

One has to lie considerably further back to get a preview for safe overtaking but a few tricks help. When someone passes you and is beginning to overtake the lorry in front this usually affords protection for you to move out for a look, if not a "follow through" overtake.

In your mirror, you may see someone overtaking a few positions behind you. This possibly means the overtaker knows the road is clear a long way ahead. Provided he has not caught up with you, and is not catching up very fast, here may be a chance for you to gradually move out and look.

The idea is offered at your own risk and care is needed not to cut in front of the overtaker behind you. You may also lean over in your seat to increase vision and make sure it is safe.

A passenger—who can drive—can be the best help.

14

MISCELLANEOUS MOTORING KNOWLEDGE

REMOVING WINDSCREEN ICE

Quickest, cheapest de-icer is a plastic scraper—it never runs out! During arctic weather de-icing washer fluid additive is indispensable. In extreme cold, freezing rain, snow or filthy spray thrown up by other vehicles can ice-up your windscreen in seconds. Maximum windscreen heat defrost is vital to warm up the glass before setting off. Keep it on, or directly you switch on your windscreen wipers, you will face a blinding smear of ice.

GUM WELLY BOOTS

Heavy boots and welly boots which can hit more than one pedal at a time and wet or muddy shoes are murder weapons. Drive in shoes, never boots. If shoes have got muddy get them cleaned off. Never be lazy! In emergency one slip—of half a second may matter.

WINDSCREEN WIPERS

Transform blade power by renewal before each winter, or every 10 15,000 miles. Twice weekly the blades need a thorough clean to get the grease off. Wipe indicators, brake and side lights and headlights while you are at it.

DISABLED DRIVERS
Superb advice and assistance is available from Automobile and Industrial Developments Ltd., Sydenham, London, S.E. 26. You need only write, or 'phone 01 778 7055 stating your particular requirements.

TYRES
By law tyres must all be suitable for the vehicle and use made of it; e.g. tyres may need to be heavy duty if a vehicle such as an estate car carries loads. Air pressures must be maintained correct and you can be in default of the law if any tyre is worn to less than one millimetre depth of tread. More than this depth must show over at least three-quarters of its width all round. The three-quarters must be in a continuous band across and there must be visible tread on the other quarter; effectively this means bald patches anywhere make a tyre illegal. No bulges or slits in the side walls are allowed, nor are cuts of more than one inch across the tread area (or of more than 10% of the tread width) permitted if they are deep enough to affect the basic body cords. Any cord showing renders a tyre illegal.

The front wheels must both have tyres of the same type (as must the back ones) and the fronts must not be radial ply unless those on the back are too. Radials on the rear wheels while cross-ply are on the front are permitted, though discouraged.

Advanced drivers would not mix types of tyre on one car at all, except perhaps during a period of changing over, because it leads to having thinner tread on the front than the back. Responsibility of the front for about 80% of braking as well as for steering and, on front wheel drive cars, for motive power is the reason.

The pattern and condition of both front tyres ideally needs to be the same, and both should be at least as new as, if not newer than, the back two tyres which again should be as new as each other.

Replace tyres too soon rather than take risks. The legal minimum of one millimetre is very thin. 2 mm might be more realistic but then endorsement and totting up for offenders would seem less reasonable.

New Tyres

New tyres need to be "run in" for a hundred miles or so. The inner beads or edges need time to settle snugly round the rim and after a "running in" period any leakage or fault will have had a chance to show. Examine and re-check pressures after a hundred miles. It is also thought that new tyres may skid slightly more easily.

"Plugged" Tubeless Tyres

Tubeless tyres are often repaired by "plugging" the puncture hole with a piece of rubber glued in. Doubt has been cast as to the long term safety of these repairs and it is strongly recommended that they be vulcanised (congealing the plug and original rubber together by heat) as soon as possible.

If you fit a tube instead of mending the hole it is essential, and garage mechanics may need reminding, to check that all the inside surface of the tyre is smooth. *Rough parts may puncture the tube.*

Damage To Tyres

Biffs against kerbs, etc., *even at parking speeds,* can cause bursts months and miles later due to unseen inside damage worsening with the flexing of the tyre in use. The sides of a tyre are extremely thin anyway; feeling the thickness of a discarded tyre will shock anyone who doesn't realise this. For the sake of your life have any tyre which has hit a kerb removed and checked.

Another point to note is how easily the "track" or alignment of the front wheels can be upset with consequent tyre wear. Fine adjustment of the track ought to be checked after any knock. It costs little. Excessive tyre squeal at corners is one sign of bad misalignment.

NURSING YOUR CAR

A little mechanical understanding helps a driver care for the needs of his car both in sickness and in health. For the novice mechanic two other titles in the Paperfront series I can recommend as a godsend: "Car Repairs Properly Explained" and the slightly more advanced "Car Doctor A–Z", both by B. C. Macdonald. Car "sympathy" as it is often called should be an integral part of a very advanced driver's professional approach.

Few things irritate an advanced driver more than when his engine misbehaves and no garage seems to be able to cure it. My experience has been that if you make sure the following are meticulously attended to on an ordinary engine you have little trouble:

1) Plugs. Clean and reset gaps each 6,000 miles, renew at 12,000.

2) Contact breaker points if fitted: Each 12,000 miles renew the points, setting the gap with fastidious accuracy. Leave well alone otherwise. Fortunately these are fast being superseded by eletronic ignition.

Fuel injection needs no owner attention and is a joy but still expensive. With carburettors, only set them yourself if expert; make sure the job is done only when (1) and (2) (where applicable) above have just been done, and, apart from topping up the piston dampers if appropriate, leave them alone. They will quite happily cover 20,000–30,000 miles without any fiddling and the setting doesn't change by itself!

3) Modern "throwaway" air cleaner elements: Turn round so a new surface faces incoming air at 9,000 miles, replace at 15,000.

* * *

CONVOY DRIVING

Suppose half-a-dozen carloads of your friends are setting off for a day out. The fastest car should be at the rear and the others arranged in order to the slowest at the front. This helps the back drivers of a fast convoy to keep up, and to catch up should they be left behind bunches of traffic which those ahead have already overtaken.

If possible agree on stopping places in advance if the journey is long. One good way is to plan that the stop shall be within the first mile out of town "so-and-so". Then all know where to look if you have been split up. The first to stop must choose an obvious and safe position which gives the others plenty of time to see and pull up— then off the road with all the cars if possible.

To enable an unplanned stop to be made (for obvious reasons!) a flash or hooting code so that the back marker can pass a message up to the front is good. Let the message percolate to the front man; he then chooses the next safe opportunity. Discuss these points with your friends before you start. Never allow your convoy to hold up other traffic trying to pass. Leave room for faster drivers to leap-frog.

TEACHING DRIVING

Despite the lobbying (by those financially concerned of course), to make non-professional driving instruction illegal, and their partial success with the passing of the law which makes it illegal to teach for payment unless qualified by a Department of Transport test, it is still a fact that of those who pass their "L" test about the same number have been taught by friends or relatives as have been near driving schools.

My earlier book "Learning To-Drive In Pictures" (uniform with this one) sets out the way to learn in a logical order through which the learner can build up complete knowledge with safety while he progresses with his practice driving in prepartion for his test.

Emergency Stops

The basic reaction "both feet down" (brake and clutch) needs to be taught during the first few hours of tuition. It is for reaction speed that the learner will be tested and which in a real emergency can save life.

Technically the clutch should not go down immediately unless the emergency occurs at very slow speed, but in my view it is madness to confuse the first day "L" driver with a two-fold rule such as "brake first—clutch down at the last second". In early days a straightforward unambiguous rule is vital. In any case as experience grows the subtle distinction of getting the clutch down later will establish itself without thought.

The quicker braking theoretically possible without pushing the clutch down is only by a tiny margin—an advantage which might be eclipsed by a fraction of a second of reaction speed being lost by uncertainty of what to do.

While some instructors may try to insist that only a clutch later technique can be right I have never heard of anyone failing their test for getting both feet down quickly. Should you get involved in teaching I suggest the first thing you establish is what may have been taught a person already in this regard. Keeping consistent, should they not have started on the "both feet down" method, would probably be better than insisting on change. It would depend what you thought of their emergency stopping ability so far.

15

ROAD SIGN AND REGULATION IDIOCY

Much excellent work is achieved in the advancement of safety by the Department of Transport, the highway engineers, and others, among whom deserving particular credit belong the majority of police. Without room to list all the good things I hope that a little criticism in what space I have left may be considered, without it appearing unduly biased!

Britain has gone sign mad. There are so many that they admit that they cannot even get them all into the Highway Code! I am certain that our excess of signs, by diverting attention (particularly speed limits where applied absurdly) and causing over-familiarity, is increasing danger especially at night. Who can remember the meaning of all these signs, duplications and variations? Many are incomprehensible without previous memorising which few people bother with as has been indicated by a number of surveys. In one recent year there were nearly 8,000 new traffic orders. One must be mentally robust to withstand them all! Too many, like those in Fig. 47, could only have been invented by desk-bound drivers!

EMOTION GRABS VOTES!

The "things are being done about roads" image has always appealed to Transport Ministers. To catch votes grand plans are as important as results. Anything which rouses emotion is wonderful, witness the 70 m.p.h. limit, the breathalyser, and the "spy in the cab" (tachometer).

The political game allows the so-called road fund (most of which never goes near the roads) to spiral upwards for ever while motorists remain disillusioned by mere promises of roads to come and frustrated by the collapse, jamming and disrepair of these here now. The fraudulent use of the "road fund" does not lose any votes because

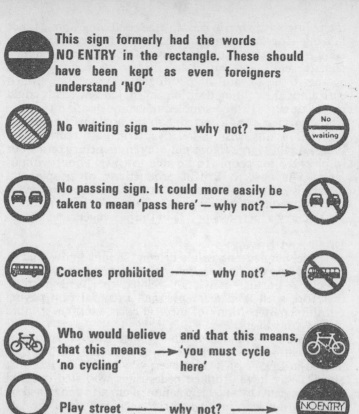

This sign formerly had the words NO ENTRY in the rectangle. These should have been kept as even foreigners understand 'NO'

No waiting sign ———— why not? ———→

No passing sign. It could more easily be taken to mean 'pass here' — why not? ———→

Coaches prohibited ——— why not? ———→

Who would believe that this means ———→ 'no cycling'

and that this means, 'you must cycle here'

Play street ——— why not? ———————→

No pedestrian sign is as bad as 'no coaches' why not have a bar crossing-out the man?

The MOT madmen really won here! Beware of airborne motorbikes presumably? It means no motor vehicles.

Fig. 47. Silly British signs.

the politicians, when asked why the road programme is not moving forward, can so easily hide behind public enquiries, conservationists, railway lobbies, the economic climate, etc. How much benefit to the country could accrue if the turmoil of pettifogging bureaucracy which surrounds the routing decisions of major new roads could be cut down? (If they doubled the compensation to those whose property was affected, half the hold-ups would melt away at a tiny cost in relative terms). It must be an unimaginably large figure not only in monetary terms but in pleasure for people to be able to travel about without jams. The cost to British productivity of people and materials sitting in queues must be vast. Yet we lavish disproportionate millions to keep jobs on defunct railways which carry a mere 5% or 6% of the passengers and goods.

Drink And Driving

Those banned for drink driving should know that if caught *again* they are probably *not insured* on any current policy. A further conviction related to a smash could therefore spell immediate personal financial ruin paying out third parties (think of medical costs, etc.) never mind loss of your licence.

It is hard to brandish meaningful statistics either pro or anti breathalyser. Nevertheless my overall feeling has altered in favour of it. However, why attack the motorist alone? Why have drunken pedestrians who step out and cause accidents escaped legislation? I am also concerned by the quantum leap in hit-and-run accidents since the law arrived coupled with unlicenced drink-drivers who give false addresses never later to be traced—a whole new level of CRIME has been fostered with all that portends for society's morals.

There is another and dangerous side to the breathalyser to ponder. It is of people (particularly the young) gulping large quantities of liquor when, if not because, they know they are having a lift. It has turned the previously harmless, even distribution of drinking for many people upside down. Whereas before they would eke out a drink or two knowing that they had to drive, now the insidious urge for bursts of heavy drinking when it is not their turn to drive has been instilled.

Who knows how much pain will be felt when alcoholism—born of the breathalyser—takes its grim toll of present day parents to the coming generation? Alcoholism continues to take gigantic strides forward.

The Poor Heavy Lorry Driver

These knights of the road and their bosses have been attacked over many years and branded like dangerous rogues. I suspect it is more the large size of vehicles and their competition with other less flexible means of carting goods which are actually the subjects of this illogical nonsense. The truth is that the heavy goods driver has the lowest accident rate per mile of any class of driver. Some years ago, spurred by a surge in the anti-lorry driver vendetta, the authorities dreamed up their heavy goods vehicle (HGV) driving test. The fact that heavy insurance premiums automatically sifted out the bad drivers was ignored with the standard cavalier disregard for reality, never mind economy. The test is rank poppycock; apart from its success in giving lots more jobs for the boys as with so many similar games, HGV licensing has now become absorbed into the social fabric. The majority of the public have become blissfully unaware of how well we got on without them or how much they are adding to the costs of industry and the inflation which has been wrecking the country.

Design Fault

Because of the tax rules vans have to be built without any side windows, not even slits. If ever a Minister of Transport was made to drive a van round London he would quickly discover how much more dangerous this nonsense makes a van to drive. He could adjust the rules at a stroke and I am sure that the present unduly high level of accidents in vans would quickly tumble.

Can Some Traffic Engineers Really Drive?

So many results of hard work by traffic engineers are a joy, it is irritating to still see some projects being completed where blunders are obvious to the driver if not to the impressively qualified engineer.

For example Fig. 48 gives an artist's impression of a new roundabout on one of the exits to the M3 as you reach it. A great crash barrier in the middle masks anything coming round the roundabout. The good sense of

Fig. 48. Badly designed crash barrier.

restraining anyone coming off the motorway too quickly and getting out of control, has been eclipsed by the daft way traffic has to pile up (sometimes literally) before it can see itself safely on to the roundabout. At least 80% of the stops caused could have been avoided simply by designing the barrier with vision in mind.

Entry slip roads on motorways and elsewhere are being built at an angle to the carriageway of about 25—30 degrees. This means drivers have to crick their necks to see themselves safely on to the inner lane while at the same time trying to build up speed and watch out for someone in front stopping unexpectedly. Many with fibrositis have to risk using mirrors alone. A 45° angle, by contrast, would not prevent adding speed and would enhance vision immediately.

Another design error but by default is the sort of junction between a small road and a high speed dual carriageway which is allowed to remain pitch dark at night. These are most commonly really dangerous just beyond the outskirts of big towns after the main dual carriageway leaves the lit urban area and drivers begin belting along plunged in darkness. What is needed but apparently not thought of, and would not be desperately expensive, is to flood the junction with light from a single giant spotlight. Accepting that drivers *do* go too fast and close to each other, particularly in rush hours, spotlights would focus their attention on the peril and show up waiting or crossing traffic. The design of the lamp and the shape of the area it lights could be standardised so that drivers automatically recognise that it means a junction well before they arrive at it.

Correct siting of lamp posts seems to receive scant attention. Along with trees, traffic lights, telegraph poles, etc., they are killers. A disproportionate number of accidents involve not vehicles with each other but crashes into solid immobile structures of this kind. Despite this being known, lamp posts are erected daily in unimaginative deadly positions. Trees are planted . . . and nurtured . . . on central reservations, roundabouts, etc. Surely it would not be difficult to set the poles 20 feet back from the road for the lamps and put the 'phone wires underground? To stop planting trees must be even easier—two friends of mine were killed recently when their car hit a pair of 4" diameter saplings—there may be an argument for retaining existing trees of great beauty but it is madness not to ban planting new ones.

It is as if some escapist passion among the bureaucrats will not recognise that cars do skid, drivers do make errors, tyres do burst, and insists (if only by default) in not allowing maximum room for these things to happen. Why do we need mammoth right angle kerb stones to bounce cars back into each other in situations where one driver gropes for the safety of the verge out of the others' way? I could go on but I probably have enough already!

CONCLUSION

I welcome readers' enquiries and criticisms and hearing of ideas you may have which might save lives if included in future editions. Please write care of my publisher enclosing a stamped addressed envelope and I will do my best to reply swiftly. I hope that readers will practise and advocate thinking and advancing! It is thinking that is crucial and not just for the other chap!

*   *   *

Permission To Quote

While this book is strictly copyright the publishers are pleased to allow anyone to use a total of up to five (5) pages from it without asking permission, *provided acknowledgement is given* thus:

"From Very Advanced Driving by A. Tom Topper (a Paperfront published by Elliot Right Way Books, Kingswood, Surrey, U.K.)."

INDEX

OUR PUBLISHING POLICY

HOW WE CHOOSE

Our policy is to consider every deserving manuscript and we can give special editorial help where an author is an authority on his subject but an inexperienced writer. We are rigorously selective in the choice of books we publish. We set the highest standards of editorial quality and accuracy. This means that a *Paperfront* is easy to understand and delightful to read. Where illustrations are necessary to convey points of detail, these are drawn up by a subject specialist artist from our panel.

HOW WE KEEP PRICES LOW

We aim for the big seller. This enables us to order enormous print runs and achieve the lowest price for you. Unfortunately, this means that you will not find in the *Paperfront* list any titles on obscure subjects of minority interest only. These could not be printed in large enough quantities to be sold for the low price at which we offer this series.

We sell almost all our *Paperfronts* at the same unit price. This saves a lot of fiddling about in our clerical departments and helps us to give you world-beating value. Under this system, the longer titles are offered at a price which we believe to be unmatched by any publisher in the world.

OUR DISTRIBUTION SYSTEM

Because of the competitive price, and the rapid turnover, *Paperfronts* are possibly the most profitable line a bookseller can handle. They are stocked by the best bookshops all over the world. It may be that your bookseller has run out of stock of a particular title. If so, he can order more from us at any time—we have a fine reputation for "same day" despatch, and we supply any order, however small (even a single copy), to any bookseller who has an account with us. We prefer you to buy from your bookseller, as this reminds him of the strong underlying public demand for *Paperfronts*. Members of the public who live in remote places, or who are housebound, or whose local bookseller is unco-operative, can order direct from us by post.

FREE

If you would like an up-to-date list of all paperfront titles currently available, send a stamped self-addressed envelope to ELLIOT RIGHT WAY BOOKS, BRIGHTON RD., LOWER KINGSWOOD, SURREY, U.K